Decoding Platform Patterns

Decoding Platform Patterns

Complete Blueprint to Harness Technology Platforms Power from Strategy to Engineering for Business Success

Shweta Vohra

Panda Innovators

Dedication

To Maa (**Sudesh**) & my silly Vohras (**Rajiv, Sanskriti & Saisha**)

Thank you for the endless Motivation, Love, and Blessings that made this book a reality.

Copyright © 2024 by Shweta Vohra

All rights reserved.

No portion of this book may be reproduced in any form without written permission from the publisher or author, except as permitted by U.S. copyright law.

This publication is designed to provide accurate and authoritative information regarding the subject matter covered. It is sold with the understanding that neither the author nor the publisher is engaged in rendering legal, investment, accounting or other professional services. While the publisher and author have used their best efforts in preparing this book, they make no representations or warranties concerning the accuracy or completeness of the contents of this book and specifically disclaim any implied warranties of merchantability or fitness for a particular purpose. No warranty may be created or extended by sales representatives or written sales materials. The advice and strategies contained herein may not be suitable for your situation. You should consult with a professional when appropriate. Neither the publisher nor the author shall be liable for any loss of profit or any other commercial damages, including but not limited to special, incidental, consequential, personal, or other damages.

Book Cover by Panda Innovators

Illustrations by Panda Innovators

First edition 2024

Contents

Foreword - From Industry Leaders	IX
Introduction	XV

Section A:
Distilling Platform Essentials

1. Navigating The Platform Dilemma	3
2. The Platforms Innovation Unfolded	19
3. Shattering Myths, Building Foundations	41
4. Simplifying Platform Definition	51

Section B:
Universal Platform Success Patterns

5. Platform Success Blueprint	63
6. Connect The Core Business Domain	75
7. Crafting Platform Strategy	91
8. Optimizing Platform Experience and Economization	111

Section C:

Platform Success Patterns - For Providers

    9. Mastering Technology Strategy and Ecosystem   129

    10. Designing Effective Platform Architecture   149

    11. Platform Development To Operations   177

Section D:

Building Legacy Through Platforms

    12. Mapping the User's Journey on the Platform   201

    13. Building Platforms: A Provider's Journey   213

    14. Case Study - Apple's Platform Patterns   227

    15. Future of Platforms with AI/ ML   251

Appendix   264

About the Author   271

Foreword - From Industry Leaders

Shweta Vohra's book *Decoding Platform Patterns* arrives at a critical juncture in the evolution of technology platforms. The Cloud Native Computing Foundation (CNCF) has long recognized the transformative power of platforms and their role as cornerstones of cloud-native computing.

Our community's work to refine a maturity model in platform engineering is founded on the belief that platforms are essential to operational efficiency and scalability in the digital landscape.

Look across the industry, and you'll see high-profile platform successes in Silicon Valley startups and established corporations.

However, their lead seems difficult to follow: a surprisingly large number of platform projects fail to make it off the drawing board, and research suggests around 80 percent.

The biggest issue is that a single agreed definition of a technology platform needs to be. Before the cloud, the phrase defined a set of on-prem, complex enterprise-class systems that provided a software infrastructure for developers, operations, and users.

The relational database was a prime example: it provided an essential set of valuable functions - storage and data processing, a development foundation for software engineers, and an API framework that third-party applications could plug in for additional functionality. One vendor controlled the code and the development roadmap.

The scale, complexity, and rate of change in the cloud have challenged both this definition of a platform *and* the practice of its development. A fresh understanding and approach are required.

The CNCF has stepped in to help. We define a platform as a collection of capabilities, documentation, and tools that support the development, deployment, operation and management of products and services. It should let organizations deliver applications and services faster and more reliably. Three characteristics define the modern platform.

First, innovation comes not from one vendor but through community-driven open source, attracting those interested in making change, finding answers, and furthering innovation. Projects generate feedback and updates at a rapid pace. The stronger the output, the more participants will be attracted, meaning technologies will become robust and sustainable.

Next, the concept of experience is a priority. Competition is intense in digital services, and customers - developers, users, or those outside your organization - have heightened expectations. Yet the cloud is a complex environment of transactions, microservices, and scale. Building a customer-first platform means organizing the components to deliver a streamlined, cohesive, and integrated experience.

Finally, we must raise our game on design, build, and work to a new platform engineering standard. As systems, infrastructure, and services mature, those designing and building platforms can harvest best practices and develop resources such as templates, meaning the platform can be scaled, operated, and secured quickly and efficiently.

This is where Shweta aligns with the vision of CNCF. With *Decoding Platform Patterns,* Shweta distils years of experience into actionable insights. Her book is grounded in her extensive work with customers on digital transformation in various sectors. She offers unbiased advice and delivers a vendor-neutral perspective applicable across different technologies.

Her book is essential because it helps simplify the otherwise complex world of platforms - a goal that resonates with the CNCF.

As you embark on your platform journey, consider Shweta's patterns and case studies. These are not theoretical concepts but tested and proven practices. Whether wishing to innovate, optimize, or simply gain a deeper understanding of platform dynamics, *Decoding Platform Patterns* is an invaluable resource.

- ***Priyanka Sharma***

Executive Director of the Cloud Native Computing Foundation (CNCF).

A leader in her field, Priyanka drives open collaboration amongst the most prominent technology players in the world through the CNCF. This non-profit organization promotes **the** *development of cloud-native computing and boasts a community of more than 220,000 contributors working on 190+ projects. She is a Stanford University graduate and a former entrepreneur who discovered a passion for developer products and whose career has seen her work with companies like Google and GitLab.*

Words from an Industry Leader

I have spent over 27 years at the forefront of technological innovation, with my journey deeply rooted in applying future technologies to create transformative solutions. Leading initiatives that harness emerging technologies such as AI and IoT to drive sustainable growth and deliver large-scale impact has been a central theme in my career. Whether it was creating the Watson Internet of Things and AI Lab in Bangalore or leading strategic engagements to develop groundbreaking projects, the essence of my work has always been about leveraging platforms to solve complex, population-scale problems.

As the first IBM Fellow in India, I had the privilege of mentoring and providing technical thought leadership within the industry during my tenure at IBM. It was a rewarding experience to guide talented professionals such as Shweta Vohra, and I am delighted to see her work come to fruition so successfully in this book.

As a fellow author, I understand the commitment and clarity of vision required to distil complex subjects into accessible, actionable insights. Having authored "AI for You - The New Game Changer," I appreciate the depth of expertise and passion that has gone into creating this book. From one author to another, I see in this work a genuine desire to guide readers through the intricacies of technology-driven platforms, making it a valuable resource.

This book is not just another addition to the growing body of literature on technology platforms. It stands out by offering a comprehensive blueprint for success, drawn from real-world experiences and lessons learned. Whether you're a seasoned technology leader or new to the field, the insights within these pages are invaluable. Shweta has done an excellent job of cutting through the noise and providing clear, actionable guidance on how to effectively build, manage, and scale platforms.

I am confident that this book will become a go-to reference for technology leaders and innovators around the world. It is a powerful tool for anyone committed to harnessing the full potential of platforms to drive growth, innovation, and long-term success.

- Shalini Kapoor

Author (AI for You - The New Gamechanger), Industry Leader & ex-IBM Fellow

Introduction

"Everywhere there can be a platform; there will be a platform." - MIT Initiative on the Digital Economy

This prediction[1] has not just come true—it has become the very fabric of our modern technological landscape. Today, almost every business either, leverages technology platforms or has evolved into a platform company itself.

Technology platforms are the engines of innovation, crafted to enhance user experiences while propelling and maximizing business success. The leading tech giants—Meta (Facebook, Instagram, WhatsApp), Apple, Microsoft, Google, Amazon, Netflix, and Tesla—serve as, prime examples of thriving digital ecosystems, all of which have become household names across the globe.

Despite their ubiquity, the concept of platforms has become increasingly muddled. The term 'platform' is now used so broadly that its true meaning often gets lost amid technological jargon and marketing hype. Studies[2] show that despite the revolutionary impact of digital platforms, over 80% of them fail. Whether it's social media, cloud services, or software infrastructures, the question remains: What exactly is a technology-driven platform? How do you know if you need one, if you have one, and if you're maximizing its effects? And how can you successfully develop and nurture one?

Given this ambiguity surrounding the concept of platforms, it's crucial to draw from real-world experience to clarify their role and impact. My journey in the Software and IT industry, spanning over two decades, has provided me with insights from serving more than 50 customers across various domains—including leading players in Telecom, Banking, Automotive, Healthcare, Travel, and Government. Through these experiences, I've witnessed the evolution of platforms firsthand.

My involvement with technology platforms began unexpectedly in 2003-2004 while developing some of the earliest web hosting solutions. Coding in Perl and Python, integrating Linux platforms, and creating templated solutions laid the groundwork for my lifelong focus on technology platforms. Those early days were marked by challenges in infrastructure and the infancy of automated builds, but they also set the stage for modern digital experiences.

Over time, I transitioned to more complex projects, including developing features for automated driving tractors in Australia—an initiative that was pioneering at the time. Subsequently, I ventured into integrations across diverse industries such as automotive, defence, IoT, and healthcare, where enterprise integration emerged as a central challenge. In the past decade I have witnessed the rise of cloud-based infrastructures, practical AI/ML implementations, and various platforms and services, fundamentally transforming our approach to technology.

The patterns and insights I've gathered over the years have become invaluable, and now I aim to share this knowledge. This book is my attempt to decode the complexities of the technology platform space, offering insights grounded in decades of hands-on experience.

As you read, picture yourself navigating these challenges and triumphs. The shifts in technology may be variables, but the underlying patterns remain constant. The stories and scenarios that follow might resonate with your own experiences, encapsulating universal challenges faced by platform companies across different domains.

Sam's Journey

To bring these experiences to life, let's merge them into one persona: Sam, a seasoned technology manager tasked with overseeing the development of a digital banking platform. This journey began with excitement and high hopes, but over four years, Sam encountered a series of challenges that tested his skills and resolve.

Year 1: Skills and Workforce Development Sam's immediate concern was equipping his team with the skills needed for new technologies. He invested heavily in training, but the steep learning curve and pressure to deliver quickly created immense challenges.

Year 2: Vendor and Support Management The complexity of the platform required collaboration with external vendors. However, issues with vendor reliability caused delays. Sam learned the importance of selecting the right partners and leveraging open-source technologies to bring in valuable resources and foster innovation.

Year 3: Technology and Platform Integration Integrating new features with legacy systems led to inefficiencies and unexpected downtime. Careful planning was required to ensure minimal disruption to operations.

Year 4: Performance, Scalability, and Cost With a rapidly growing user base, scalability became a priority. Sam had to implement solutions to maintain performance under increased demand.

Throughout those four years, there have been continuous barriers, the most prevalent of which are the following:

Ongoing: Security, Compliance, and Risk Management As the platform matured, ensuring security and compliance with regulations became critical. This required constant vigilance to protect user data and meet regulatory requirements.

Ongoing: User Adoption and Customer Impact User acceptance was key to the platform's success. Sam focused on ensuring the platform was user-friendly and communicated new features clearly to build trust.

Ongoing: Strategic and Operational Impact Implementing new technologies often disrupted daily operations, but Sam knew these challenges were essential for long-term growth. Aligning the platform with the company's strategic goals was crucial.

These challenges are not unique to Sam. His experiences are reflective of the broader challenges faced by technology managers in today's fast-evolving digital landscape. Does everyone in the industry need to go through the same years-long cycle before realizing the true potential of platforms and avoiding failure? Could Sam's journey and those of others in similar circumstances have been easier? This book decodes these pain points through a comprehensive 'Platform Success Blueprint,' guiding readers step by step and enriching the experience with a leading technology company's platform case study.

Who Is This Book For?

If you are responsible for driving innovation and scaling your business through platforms within your organization, whether through leadership, design, or engineering, this book is your strategic guide. What sets this book apart is its focus on practical, hands-on advice, drawn from real-world experiences and enriched with many examples of companies operating in this space. It provides actionable insights and offers a chance to learn from both their successes and failures. Staying ahead in digital transformation requires not just keeping up but mastering the patterns that define successful platforms.

This book is for those who are:

- Leading platform strategy and development within their business.

- Designing and implementing technology-driven platforms.

- Navigating complex technological landscapes.

Just like Sam, if you're leading platform strategy, designing technology-driven platforms, or navigating complex technological landscapes whether for internal use or an external business platform, this book will serve as your essential resource. The real-world scenarios in this book will equip you with the tools to understand, master, and excel in platform technology patterns.

How to Read This Book

This book is a comprehensive resource filled with real-world examples, patterns of success and failure, and balanced insights. It's packed with practical advice and illustrative examples intricately woven throughout the chapters. The structure is designed to gradually build your understanding, beginning with foundational concepts and progressing to more advanced topics. This ensures you have the necessary knowledge to tackle each phase of platform usage and development.

This isn't just a book to read once; it's meant to be a reference guide throughout your platform journey, whether you're building a business, an external-facing platform, or an internal developer platform. Consider it your companion on the intricate journey of platform development, helping you navigate the evolving landscape of technology platforms and leverage them to your advantage.

As you progress through the chapters, I encourage you to actively apply the strategies discussed, turning insights into action. Keep this book close as a constant reference, offering guidance and support whenever needed.

Here's a guide to the book's structure:

- **Section A:** Establishes essential definitions and a shared understanding for everyone involved with technology platforms.

- **Section B:** Delves into universal platform success patterns, progressing into in-depth technical examples and implementations, making it equally applicable to any level of platform user or provider.

- **Section C:** Focuses on the challenges and solutions specifically for platform providers, covering aspects of technology, design, and development in greater depth.

- **Section D:** Explores platform journeys, concluding with a detailed case study that is equally applicable for both users and providers to learn from as they prepare for the next wave of platforms.

This book is not just a tool for learning but also a gateway to a larger community of innovators and platform enthusiasts. As you delve into the concepts and strategies presented, you'll find that the journey of platform development is enriched by collaboration and shared experiences.

With that in mind, I invite you to join our vibrant community, where you can connect with like-minded individuals, learn from experts, and share your own experiences. We value your feedback, so please don't hesitate to reach out at connect@pandainnovators.com. To become part of this community and stay updated with the latest insights, simply enrol here at https://pandainnovators.com. We look forward to welcoming you!

Enjoy the read!

---

1. https://ide.mit.edu/insights/just-released-2018-platform-strategy-report/
2. https://www.itm-conferences.org/articles/itmconf/abs/2023/01/itmconf_iess2023_05001/itmconf_iess2023_05001.html

Section A

Distilling Platform Essentials

Chapter One

Navigating The Platform Dilemma

"Technology platform's public triumphs often mask private frustrations."

Platforms are a powerful fusion of technology and business, reshaping industries and consumer experiences while driving strategic growth. Yet, with their immense potential, significant challenges also arise. As platforms expand, the complexities of their implementation and management also increase. Navigating these complexities with a clear understanding of both opportunities and pitfalls is crucial to avoiding common missteps and ensuring long-term success.

Among entrepreneurs and investors, platform-based businesses have gained significant popularity, with 60% to 70% of 2017's unicorns, including companies like Uber and Airbnb, operating as platforms[1]. However, their success is not guaranteed; like traditional companies, they must outperform competitors and remain socially and politically viable to avoid regulatory and financial risks. Despite the popularity of platforms, the challenges they face are significant and demand careful management.

In the fast-paced tech landscape, stories of public triumph often contrast sharply with internal struggles. While platforms are often celebrated as revolutionary, they frequently fall short of expectations, leading to numerous challenges. Misunderstood or oversold technologies blur the vision, break expectations, and result in increased effort with diminished returns. Consider my experience with an automotive company, where I led a dedicated agile team of 20 developers and testers tasked with creating a cutting-edge application platform. The project began with great enthusiasm—"Wow, all hail Microservices!" For over two years, we toiled to craft a Minimum Viable Product (MVP) using modern platforms, cloud services, and off-the-shelf solutions. Just as we were on the verge of a breakthrough, a new technology emerged, promising faster, more efficient results—a better fit for our needs. We faced a dilemma: continue with our in-house platform work or pivot to the new, promising technology. This experience underscored the internal challenges that often accompany platform development, where the excitement of innovation can be tempered by the realities of technological churn and shifting priorities.

There are countless instances where platforms are misunderstood, oversold, or hyped beyond their capacity. This misalignment leads to unmet expectations, misinterpreted technologies, faulty integrations, and products that fail to deliver on their promises.

Real-World Examples and Insights

Let's explore real-world examples highlighting the critical need for a discerning approach to adopting platform technologies. These examples are not just illustrative; they are crucial learning tools that provide practical insights into platform development and deployment realities. Drawing from my own experiences and interviews with industry leaders, these cases emphasize the importance of looking beyond marketing hype to truly evaluate a technology's capabilities and limitations.

As you read, consider which of these situations resonate with your experiences. Understanding these challenges is essential for successfully navigating the complexities of the platform landscape.

Example 1: CTOs often voice concerns with the relentless churn of platforms and services. In a world where technology evolves at breakneck speed, keeping pace feels like a mammoth task. Yet, they cannot afford to ignore these rapid advancements: One CTO admitted, 'If I don't keep up, I'll fall behind. Sometimes we're just pretending to understand everything, while our designers and developers are equally in the dark.'

Example 2: An Engineering Manager shared the challenges of adopting and integrating new technology into an existing platform, hoping to enhance operations and efficiency. Initially, the platform seemed promising, a perfect fit for their needs. However, as implementation progressed, the vendor failed to deliver on scalability requirements. This left teams grappling with incomplete documentation and poorly integrated solutions, leading to operational inefficiencies and frustration. This experience underscored the importance of thorough vetting and realistic assessment of platform capabilities before committing to ensure alignment with long-term needs and growth potential.

Example 3: Technology Architects frequently encounter the challenge of integrating the new with the old. The struggle isn't in building the platform but in finding the right balance. Common questions asked by architects include: Is this new technology hype or reality? Is it sustainable in the long term? How will it integrate with our existing systems? And when partners make promises—is that just marketing buzz or genuine potential?

Example 4: A Platform Financial Administrator expressed growing concerns over FinOps. As organizations increasingly adopt cloud-based solutions, managing and optimizing cloud costs while ensuring financial accountability becomes critical. Balancing innovation with financial prudence adds yet another layer of complexity to the decision-making process.

Example 5: A Business Manager at a telecom company reflected, 'Our current platforms perform well and efficiently support our systems. The real question is—will this new, promising technology truly work for us? For example, our legacy CRM system has been reliable and effective for years. Introducing a new platform might offer advanced features, but we need to carefully assess whether it will genuinely benefit us or risk disrupting our operations.'

Example 6: A Software Engineer shared his experience: 'I never anticipated that my skill set would become obsolete so quickly in the world of digital platforms. For instance, my expertise in traditional database management was once highly valued, but now, with the rise of cloud-based solutions and NoSQL databases, it feels outdated. Every new development brings yet another advancement—it's challenging, but also quite exciting.'

Example 7: A Product Manager encountered challenges when their platform's user experience was compromised, despite its technical robustness. The platform struggled with user adoption due to a poorly designed interface and cumbersome workflows, ultimately leading to high customer churn.

Example 8: A Compliance Officer struggled to ensure that the platform adhered to evolving regulations, such as GDPR or industry-specific compliance requirements. The introduction of new technologies often complicated these efforts, as existing platforms may not have been designed with these regulations in mind. At the same time old regulatory practices and processes block the pace that is possible with new.

Example 9: A Head of IT expressed concern about becoming too dependent on a single vendor's ecosystem, which makes it challenging to switch providers or integrate with other technologies without incurring significant costs or operational disruptions. Vendor lock-in is a major issue, especially as companies increasingly rely on cloud services and specific vendor technologies.

Analyzing the Key Learnings and Opportunities

The insights mentioned above from various levels of platform engagement lead us to the following observations, which represent both learnings and opportunities to change the course:

- **Misaligned Expectations:** A common issue with platform technologies is the gap between promises and actual delivery. Companies often invest heavily in platforms, expecting seamless integrations and transformative capabilities. However, unmet expectations can lead to frustration and wasted resources. For instance, a major retail company might invest in a new e-commerce platform, expecting increased sales and customer engagement, only to discover that the platform's capabilities were overstated, leading to a complex integration process that hinders progress.

- **Misunderstood Technologies:** Technological innovations are inherently complex, and a lack of understanding can result in their misapplication. A typical scenario involves adopting a platform without fully grasping its limitations and requirements, leading to underutilized features or a total mismatch with company needs. Imagine a company adopting a cloud-native platform to modernize its operations. However, due to incompatible features and a lack of adequate training and customization, the development teams struggle to navigate the platform efficiently. This leads to deployment delays, integration issues with legacy systems, and overall decreased productivity, ultimately undermining the potential benefits of the cloud-native approach.

- **Broken Integrations:** Seamless integration is a major selling point for many platforms, but in practice, this can be difficult to achieve. Broken integrations often cause disruptions and inefficiencies. Consider a logistics company deploying a new supply chain management platform. Despite promises of smooth integration with existing systems, incompatibilities arise, leading to frequent breakdowns, manual workarounds, and ultimately, increased operational costs.

- **Shallow Products or Promises:** The rush to capitalize on the latest technology trends can result in products that are not fully developed or robust enough for practical use. These shallow products often fail to meet the demands of real-world applications. For example, a financial services firm might adopt a new blockchain-based platform touted for its security and transparency. However, the platform's immaturity leads to operational challenges, regulatory issues, and a loss of trust from clients.

The variety and complexity of platforms and related technologies can be overwhelming, making it challenging for organizations to stay ahead. The real question isn't just about keeping up with ever-evolving platform technologies; it's about uncovering the opportunities within the platform industry and understanding if these technologies are truly designed to meet the needs of businesses or if they require a different approach to maximize their potential.

Does this resonate with you? Is your organization navigating these challenges, or are you, as a user or provider, exploring ways to align platform technologies more effectively with your goals? If so, let's embark on a journey together to decode these complexities, understand the underlying patterns, and uncover the best practices that can help you navigate the intricate world of platform technologies with greater clarity and confidence.

Let's Assess Your Platform Story

Before we dive deeper into platform patterns and strategies, it's crucial to assess your current platform situation and story. This assessment will serve as a map, guiding you through this book and its chapters more effectively. By tailoring these insights to your specific context, you'll find the guidance in this book even more relevant and actionable.

Over the years, I've had countless conversations about platform technologies and the ways of working around them—at conferences, in office meetings, during client engagements, and with technology providers and users alike. Having experienced these challenges firsthand, both as a platform provider and a user, I was inspired to write this book and share these insights.

Now, it's your turn. Before we can build a dialogue, we need to establish a strong foundation. Let's acknowledge that certain truths apply to most companies dealing with platform technologies, regardless of scale. Perhaps one of these experiences mirrors your journey or that of the organization you work for.

To personalize the insights and takeaways from this book to your specific context, let's start with a small exercise. Be honest with yourself as you reflect on the questions below. This exercise is designed for self-reflection and will help you maximize the value you get from this book.

Take a moment to consider the following questions. Indicate the level of concern or criticality in your context by marking each as **H-High, M-Medium, or L-Low**, based on how relatable it is to your situation. Your responses should reflect your role, apprehensions, and challenges, helping to create a clear path forward as we explore platform journeys together.

1. What are the risks of this platform, and how can they be mitigated?

2. How flexible is the platform for our (customers') needs?

3. What if this implementation takes longer than expected?

4. How secure is this new platform?

5. What kind of support will we receive post-implementation?

6. What is our strategy for continuous platform improvement and innovation?

7. How will this platform enhance user experience and ensure high adoption rates?

8. What is our exit strategy if this technology does not work out?

9. Will this technology help us stay compliant with regulations?

10. How does this technology fit into our overall technology roadmap?

11. How do we manage the risks associated with this technology?

12. How will this technology enhance our customer strategy?

13. How secure is our data on this platform?

14. How do we get internal buy-in for this change?

15. Is there sufficient documentation for our developers?

16. How do we plan to scale our platform to support a growing user base?

17. Will our customers adapt to this new change (platform features)?

18. Is this technology too complex for our team to manage?

19. Can this technology provide us with a competitive advantage?

20. Is the market for this technology stable?

21. Will this actually improve our operational efficiency?

22. Is platform scalable for future growth and technological advancements?

23. What is the return on investment for this new technology?

24. How can we better help users integrate our platform with their existing systems?

25. How do we manage vendor lock-in and dependencies?

26. How do we continuously develop skills for new technologies?

27. Can we justify the cost of this technology?

28. How will this platform improve our overall technology stack?

29. How challenging will data migration be?

30. How well does this platform align with our overall business strategy and long-term goals?

31. How expensive will it be to train our staff?

32. What is the vendor's future strategy, and how do we communicate our platform's plans to users?

33. How will we manage the transition to this new system?

34. How do we ensure our platform remains competitive in the market?

35. How will our customers perceive this change?

36. How will this new technology integrate with our legacy systems?

37. Can I trust this vendor to deliver on their promises?

38. What is the realistic timeframe for implementation?

39. Are we ready for a long-term commitment to this technology?

40. Will this technology perform well under heavy workload?

41. How robust is the backup and recovery process?

42. What metrics will we use to measure the success and adoption of our platform?

After identifying your concerns as given above, focus on those marked as "H - High". Jot these down and refer to Appendix A at the end of this book to categorize your pain points and determine where your immediate attention is needed. By prioritizing what's most critical, you'll be better equipped to navigate the platform landscape effectively, ensuring that your efforts yield the best possible outcomes for your organization. As you continue through the following chapters, this foundation of critical evaluation and prioritization will be essential. Each chapter will build upon certain principles, offering deeper insights and strategies to help you navigate the complex world of platform technologies with confidence and clarity.

Platforms are complex systems, often compared to intricate puzzles with many interdependent pieces. This complexity can slow down progress and make innovation challenging. However, the platform success blueprint outlined in this book is designed to help you navigate these challenges holistically, empowering you to amplify your platform's potential at any stage of your journey.

Now, let's explore the decades of platform innovation that have shaped today's landscape in the next chapter.

Key Takeaways

- Platforms drive innovation and growth but come with significant challenges that must be effectively managed for long-term success.

- Critically evaluate platform technologies beyond marketing promises to ensure they align with your organization's needs and goals.

- Assess your organization's current situation and challenges to prioritize issues and make informed, strategic decisions in your platform journey.

---

1. https://sloanreview.mit.edu/article/the-future-of-platforms/

Chapter Two

The Platforms Innovation Unfolded

"When you truly understand the problem, the solution becomes a matter of time."

We're witnessing a surge in platforms and the complexities that accompany them. This naturally leads to the question: What's the big deal? Digital transformation has been a long-standing journey, beginning long before it became a buzzword. Each phase of this journey has introduced new tools and paradigms that have reshaped how businesses operate and innovate. The cycle of outdated technology being replaced by innovations is nothing new. So, what makes platforms particularly challenging in today's landscape?

To grasp these challenges, we must step back and examine the underlying causes. Is the problem genuine, or is it simply a misconception?

Four key forces have accelerated the pace of change and innovation, pushing us toward rapid, granular advancements. The internet, the most significant enabler, has expanded global reach and fuelled unprecedented innovation. Users unconsciously or implicitly demand better experiences and greater value, while creators strive for innovation, differentiation, and growth. This dynamic perpetuates a continuous cycle of innovation, demand, and further evolution.

But what exactly are these four forces?

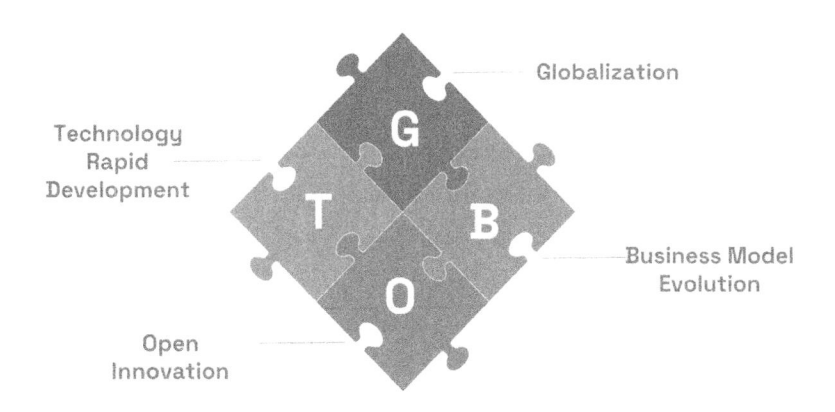

- Globalization
- Technology Rapid Development
- Business Model Evolution
- Open Innovation

Globalization

The internet has dismantled geographical barriers, allowing businesses to innovate and operate globally. This global reach requires platforms that can serve diverse markets with varied needs. Globalization has reshaped the technology landscape, enabling global operation, networking, and scaling. Key drivers include the strengthening of the internet backbone, advancements in networking infrastructure, and increased connectivity. Simultaneously, decentralization has extended reach and scale, influencing working cultures and governance models.

One of the most significant impacts of digital transformation is the shift towards decentralized working cultures and governance models. This shift, characterized by remote work, collaboration tools, and distributed governance, has accelerated the acceptance of innovation and changed how businesses operate globally.

Business Models Explosion

The rise of new business models, particularly those driven by digital platforms, has expanded the scope of what businesses can offer and how they engage with customers. Platforms have evolved beyond the traditional B2B (Business-to-business) and B2C (Business-to-consumer) models, leading to an explosion of service models and platforms.

- C2C (Consumer to Consumer): Platforms like Airbnb, eBay, and Uber enable consumers to exchange services or products directly.

- C2M (Consumer to Manufacturer): Platforms like Alibaba and Nike By You allow consumers to directly influence or order from manufacturers.

- D2D (Developer to Developer): GitHub and Stack Overflow facilitate collaboration, resource sharing, and problem-solving among developers.

- H2H (Human to Human): LinkedIn and Facebook foster direct interactions and collaboration between individuals, enhancing both personal and professional connections.

These business models (and many more, as detailed in Appendix B) have given rise to numerous platforms and platform companies. To such an extent, they have impacted everyone's life in one way or another.

Open Innovation

Open innovation, fuelled by open-source projects and community-driven developments, has accelerated technological progress. However, this openness also brings challenges, particularly in integrating a diverse range of technologies and innovations.

Open source has unlocked unprecedented opportunities for contribution, innovation, and acceleration in the tech industry. It's a powerful force, simultaneously driving progress and adding complexity to the platform economy. With countless contributors and industry-backed projects, open-source initiatives are pushing major advancements in infrastructure, security, cloud-native technologies, AI, ML, and more. Organizations like the Linux Foundation, Apache Software Foundation, Free Software Foundation (FSF), and initiatives like Open Standards channel this innovation into the ecosystem, while also adding layers of complexity.

To further accelerate the pace and simplify the heavy lifting of setting up and maintaining infrastructure and operation. birth of cloud-based infrastructure services emerged. As cloud and cloud-native technologies gained momentum, tools and platforms evolved rapidly, with Kubernetes emerging in 2014 as a cornerstone of this ecosystem. Since its introduction, the container orchestration landscape has expanded exponentially, with over 180 projects now under the Cloud Native Computing Foundation (CNCF). While these projects enhance various functionalities, they also introduce significant challenges in managing and integrating these tools effectively.

Rapid Technological Development

The rapid pace of technological advancement, from cloud computing to artificial intelligence, demands platforms that are both adaptable and scalable. This evolution pressures businesses to stay current with emerging technologies and integrate them effectively into their operations.

Understanding the breadth and depth of this evolution can be daunting. However, by examining key areas such as programming languages, database technologies, and virtualization technologies across different decades, we can appreciate the scale and acceleration of technological progress.

a) Evolution of Programming Languages

The evolution of programming languages reflects the ongoing advancements in technology, with each decade bringing new languages designed to address emerging challenges and improve developer productivity. From early languages like COBOL and Fortran to modern languages like Kotlin and TypeScript, this progression highlights continuous innovation in software development. Take a look at the illustrations to see the continuous evolution and impact of these languages over time.

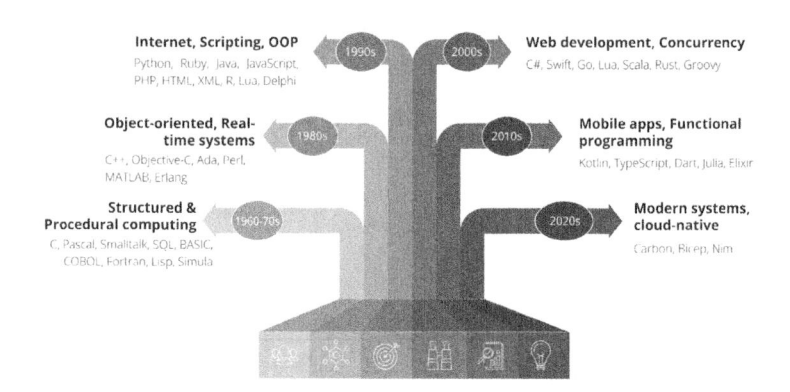

Internet, Scripting, OOP (1990s)
Python, Ruby, Java, JavaScript, PHP, HTML, XML, R, Lua, Delphi

Web development, Concurrency (2000s)
C#, Swift, Go, Lua, Scala, Rust, Groovy

Object-oriented, Real-time systems (1980s)
C++, Objective-C, Ada, Perl, MATLAB, Erlang

Mobile apps, Functional programming (2010s)
Kotlin, TypeScript, Dart, Julia, Elixir

Structured & Procedural computing (1960-70s)
C, Pascal, Smalltalk, SQL, BASIC, COBOL, Fortran, Lisp, Simula

Modern systems, cloud-native (2020s)
Carbon, Bicep, Nim

b) Evolution of Database Technologies

Over the decades, database technologies have evolved significantly, transforming from early hierarchical and network models to modern distributed and cloud-native databases. Each decade has brought new advancements, addressing the growing needs for scalability, flexibility, and performance in data management. This progression highlights the continuous innovation in database systems to meet the demands of ever-expanding data environments. Refer to the illustration below to see this evolution in detail.

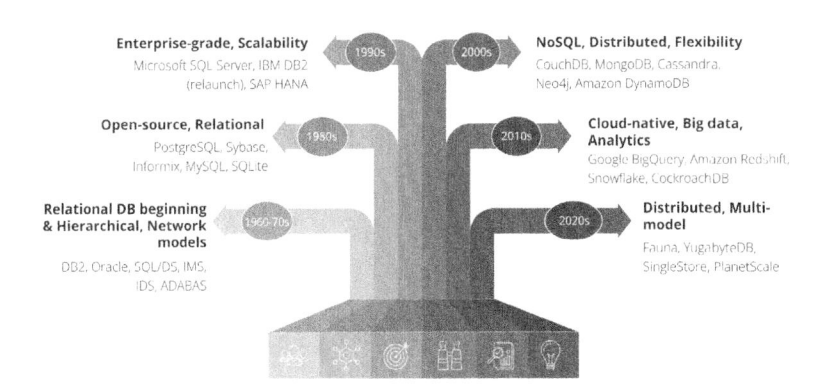

Enterprise-grade, Scalability (1990s)
Microsoft SQL Server, IBM DB2 (relaunch), SAP HANA

Open-source, Relational (1980s)
PostgreSQL, Sybase, Informix, MySQL, SQLite

Relational DB beginning & Hierarchical, Network models (1960-70s)
DB2, Oracle, SQL/DS, IMS, IDS, ADABAS

NoSQL, Distributed, Flexibility (2000s)
CouchDB, MongoDB, Cassandra, Neo4j, Amazon DynamoDB

Cloud-native, Big data, Analytics (2010s)
Google BigQuery, Amazon Redshift, Snowflake, CockroachDB

Distributed, Multi-model (2020s)
Fauna, YugabyteDB, SingleStore, PlanetScale

c) Evolution of Virtualization Technologies

Virtualization technologies have drastically evolved, starting from basic mainframe virtual machines to advanced containerization and microservices orchestration platforms. Each decade has introduced new tools and methods to optimize resource utilization, enhance scalability, and improve the deployment of applications across diverse environments. This evolution reflects the industry's growing need for flexible, efficient, and scalable computing solutions. Refer to the illustration below to see this progression in detail.

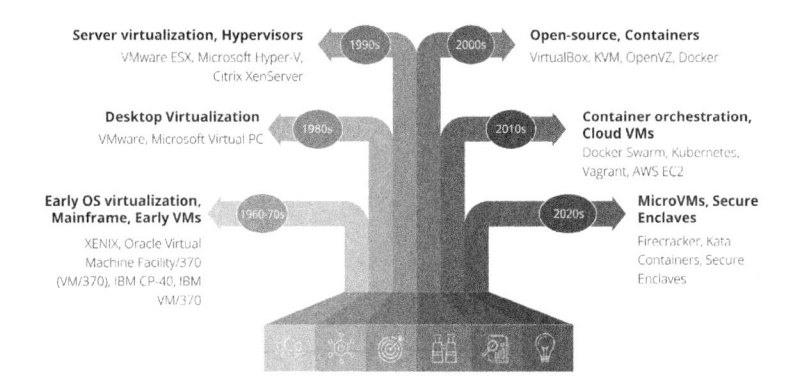

Server virtualization, Hypervisors (1990s)
VMware ESX, Microsoft Hyper-V, Citrix XenServer

Desktop Virtualization (1980s)
VMware, Microsoft Virtual PC

Early OS virtualization, Mainframe, Early VMs (1960-70s)
XENIX, Oracle Virtual Machine Facility/370 (VM/370), IBM CP-40, IBM VM/370

Open-source, Containers (2000s)
VirtualBox, KVM, OpenVZ, Docker

Container orchestration, Cloud VMs (2010s)
Docker Swarm, Kubernetes, Vagrant, AWS EC2

MicroVMs, Secure Enclaves (2020s)
Firecracker, Kata Containers, Secure Enclaves

With each passing decade, the pace of technological innovation accelerates, offering an ever-expanding array of tools and options. This progression elevates technology along the value chain, simplifying many tasks while also introducing challenges in adoption speed, skill development, and technology management.

Organizations must now navigate a complex and ever-changing landscape, making strategic decisions about which technologies to adopt and how to integrate them effectively. The rapid evolution also underscores the importance of continuous learning and adaptability within teams to maintain competitiveness and leverage new opportunities

Platform Trends – Over Years

As we explore the trends that have shaped today's platform economy, it will become clear how various forces converged to strengthen this ecosystem. By examining historical and technological developments, you'll gain a deeper understanding of how different contexts mixed and evolved into the complex platform landscape we see today.

To fully grasp platform evolution and its underlying patterns, we need to delve into the history of technology and how platforms have developed over time. This exploration will help identify key trends and the forces that have driven the rapid development and adoption of platforms across industries. While you read next page for certain prominent platform trends. **Take a moment to recall** the first few platforms you interacted with—what stands out? How did they shape your understanding of technology?

Platform Trends - Over Years

Decades	Early	Mid	Late
2000	**Search Engines** - Google, Yahoo, Bing. **E-commerce** - Amazon, eBay. **Social Networking** - Friendster, MySpace. **Content Management** - WordPress, Drupal.	**Blogging** - Blogger, Tumblr. **Online Music** - Pandora, Last.fm. **Prof. Networking** - Monster, LinkedIn. **Video Sharing** - YouTube.	**Microblogging** - Twitter. **App Stores** - Apple App Store, Google Play. **Cloud Computing** - AWS, Google Cloud. **Mobile OS** - iOS, Android.
2010	**Photo Sharing** - Instagram, Pinterest. **Collaborative Consumption** - Airbnb, Uber. **Streaming Services** - Netflix, Spotify. **Enterprise Collaboration** - Slack, Trello.	**Messaging Apps** - WhatsApp, Messenger. **Ride Sharing** - Lyft. **Online Marketplaces** - Etsy, Alibaba. **Wearable Tech** - Fitbit, Apple Watch.	**Smart Home** - Amazon Echo, Google Home. **Augmented Reality** - Pokémon GO, AR Lense. **Virtual Reality** - Oculus Rift, HTC Vive. **AI & ML Platforms** - Azure AI, Sagemaker.
2020	**Video Conferencing** - Zoom, MS Teams. **Health Tech** - Peloton, Telehealth. **Remote Work Collaboration** - Asana. **Short-form Videos** - TikTok, Insta Reels.	**Decentralized Finance** - Ethereum, Uniswap. **Cryptocurrency** - Coinbase, Binance. **NFT Marketplaces** - OpenSea, Rarible. **Autonomous Vehicles** - Tesla, Waymo.	**Metaverse** - Meta, Decentraland. **AI/ ML** - ChatGPT (OpenAI), DALL-E. **Blockchain** - Ethereum 2.0, Hyperledger. **Quantum Computing** - IBM, Google. Continuing to Evolve or Mature in this Space

The Changing Landscape of Platforms and Technology

Over the past several decades, the landscape of platforms and technology has undergone profound changes, driven by relentless innovation and the evolving needs of businesses. Let's squeeze out the gist of platforms and tech innovation from the 1960s to the 2020s, decade by decade. With the illustrations provided, you'll be amazed to discover that some challenges we face today have persisted for decades, while other technologies that seem seamless now have rapidly evolved and shaped the industry in remarkable ways.

In the 1960s

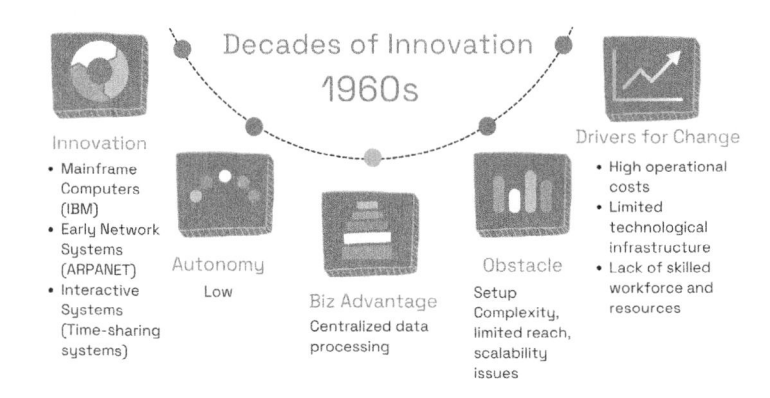

Decades of Innovation — 1960s

Innovation
- Mainframe Computers (IBM)
- Early Network Systems (ARPANET)
- Interactive Systems (Time-sharing systems)

Autonomy
Low

Biz Advantage
Centralized data processing

Obstacle
Setup Complexity, limited reach, scalability issues

Drivers for Change
- High operational costs
- Limited technological infrastructure
- Lack of skilled workforce and resources

Businesses faced significant challenges, leading to higher failure rates. High operational costs were a primary hurdle, as the technology of the time required substantial investment even for basic automation. The technological infrastructure was also limited, preventing companies from relying on advanced systems to streamline operations or improve efficiency. Compounding these issues was a lack of a skilled workforce; rapid technological advancements outpaced the available training and education, leaving many businesses unable to fully grasp or implement the new technologies. The concept of technology platforms was virtually nonexistent due to minimal autonomy in systems. Expertise in effectively managing and implementing new technologies was scarce. Each decade brought progress, and in this era, the main drivers of change were limited technological infrastructure and high operational costs.

In The 1970s

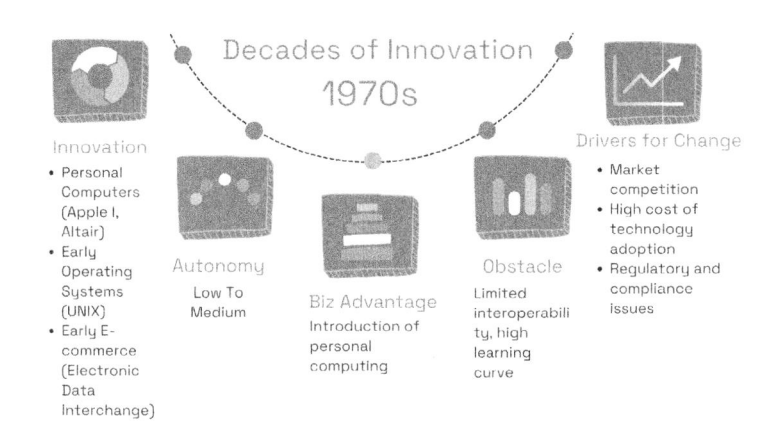

Decades of Innovation 1970s

Innovation
- Personal Computers (Apple I, Altair)
- Early Operating Systems (UNIX)
- Early E-commerce (Electronic Data Interchange)

Autonomy
Low To Medium

Biz Advantage
Introduction of personal computing

Obstacle
Limited interoperability, high learning curve

Drivers for Change
- Market competition
- High cost of technology adoption
- Regulatory and compliance issues

The business landscape began to shift significantly. This decade marked a major step forward with the advent of personal computers and the initial stages of platforms, particularly through standardising operating system functions. Autonomy increased from low to medium levels, giving businesses more technological control. However, companies still faced substantial challenges. Market competition intensified as more players entered various industries, driving a constant need for innovation and differentiation. The high cost of adopting new technologies continued to be a barrier, requiring significant investment for companies to remain competitive. Additionally, regulatory and compliance issues became more prominent, as governments worldwide introduced new laws to regulate business practices and protect consumers. This increased the complexity and cost of doing business, particularly for companies that struggled to adapt quickly to new regulations. These developments set the stage for the next decade, where the pace of innovation accelerated, particularly in terms of standardization.

In The 1980s

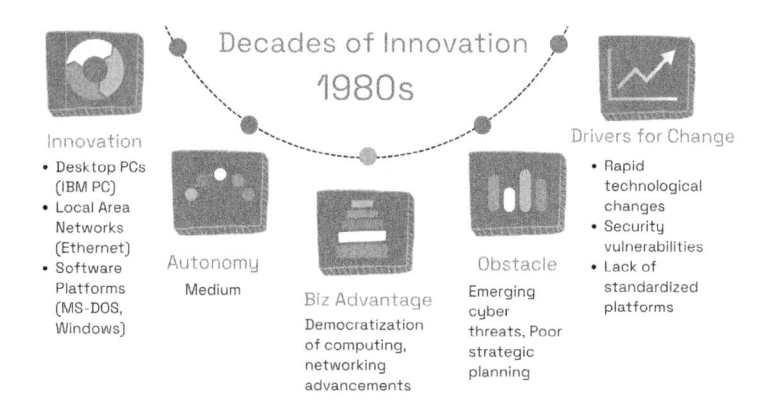

Decades of Innovation — 1980s

Innovation
- Desktop PCs (IBM PC)
- Local Area Networks (Ethernet)
- Software Platforms (MS-DOS, Windows)

Autonomy
Medium

Biz Advantage
Democratization of computing, networking advancements

Obstacle
Emerging cyber threats, Poor strategic planning

Drivers for Change
- Rapid technological changes
- Security vulnerabilities
- Lack of standardized platforms

The 1980s saw the introduction of software platforms that advanced autonomy to a medium level, marked by the emergence of desktop PCs, local area networks, and software-based platforms like MS-DOS and Windows. However, this decade also brought new challenges, particularly in the form of cyber attacks. Rapid technological changes characterized the era, forcing businesses to continuously upgrade their systems to keep pace with innovation. This accelerated pace often exposed security vulnerabilities, as new technologies were implemented faster than they could be properly secured. Additionally, poor strategic planning became a common issue, with companies struggling to accurately anticipate market trends and technological advancements. This lack of foresight led many businesses to invest in technologies or strategies that quickly became obsolete or ineffective, contributing to their downfall. These developments set the stage for the 1990s, a decade that would further accelerate technological change.

In The 1990s

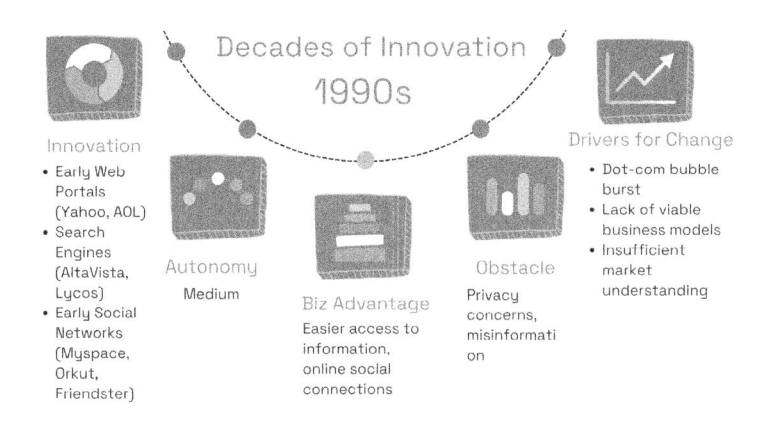

Decades of Innovation 1990s

Innovation
- Early Web Portals (Yahoo, AOL)
- Search Engines (AltaVista, Lycos)
- Early Social Networks (Myspace, Orkut, Friendster)

Autonomy
Medium

Biz Advantage
Easier access to information, online social connections

Obstacle
Privacy concerns, misinformation

Drivers for Change
- Dot-com bubble burst
- Lack of viable business models
- Insufficient market understanding

The 1990s were marked by the rise and fall of the dot-com bubble. This decade saw the emergence of new ways to democratize business, with business models evolving from traditional B2B to more consumer-focused B2C approaches. Businesses began to realize the value of easy access to information and online social connections, leading to the creation of platforms such as Yahoo, Myspace, Friendster, and AOL, which were designed for broader public reach. However, the tech sector faced significant setbacks when the speculative bubble burst, leading to the failure of many businesses. A lack of viable business strategy was a major factor, as numerous startups prioritized rapid growth and market presence over sustainable profitability. Additionally, insufficient market understanding resulted in misaligned products and services that either failed to meet consumer needs or never gained public attention. Companies that had heavily invested in internet-based ventures struggled to adapt when the bubble burst, leading to widespread business failures. In hindsight, the dot-com burst served as a necessary correction, ultimately driving the next wave of innovation.

In The 2000s

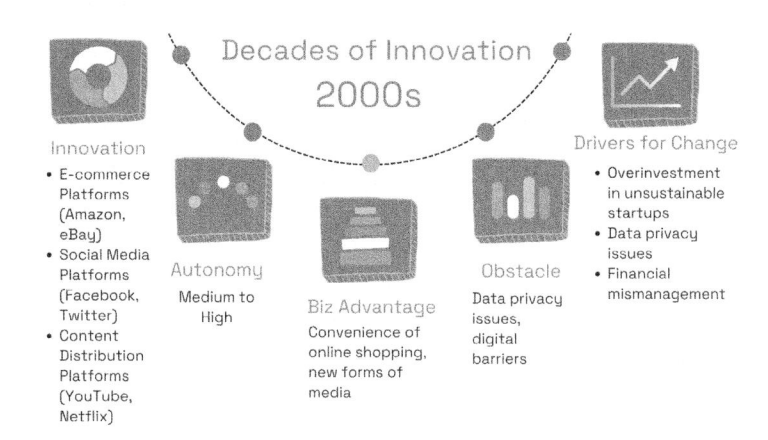

Decades of Innovation — 2000s

Innovation
- E-commerce Platforms (Amazon, eBay)
- Social Media Platforms (Facebook, Twitter)
- Content Distribution Platforms (YouTube, Netflix)

Autonomy
Medium to High

Biz Advantage
Convenience of online shopping, new forms of media

Obstacle
Data privacy issues, digital barriers

Drivers for Change
- Overinvestment in unsustainable startups
- Data privacy issues
- Financial mismanagement

The 2000s witnessed a surge in platform-based businesses, marking the beginning of a broader understanding of platforms and their economic growth potential. Key players like Meta (formerly Facebook), Twitter, YouTube, and Netflix began bringing medium to high autonomy not only to businesses but also to individuals capable of leveraging technology. Open source and standardization played a crucial role during this period, with projects like Linux and the adoption of web standards enabling greater interoperability and innovation across platforms. However, this period was also marked by overinvestment in unsustainable startups, driven by the optimism of the preceding decade's tech boom. At the same time, concerns over data privacy grew, as businesses faced new challenges in protecting customer information amidst increasing cyber threats. Financial mismanagement became a critical issue, with many companies failing to maintain proper oversight of their finances, leading to unsustainable business practices and eventual failure. The financial crisis of 2008 further exacerbated these problems, causing a significant downturn in the global economy and contributing to widespread business failures. These challenges led to greater maturity in the platform space and set the stage for significant changes in the following decade.

In The 2010s

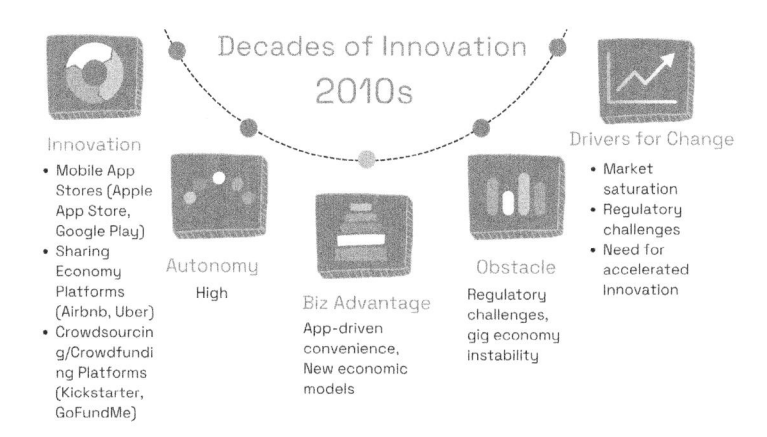

Decades of Innovation 2010s

Innovation
- Mobile App Stores (Apple App Store, Google Play)
- Sharing Economy Platforms (Airbnb, Uber)
- Crowdsourcing/Crowdfunding Platforms (Kickstarter, GoFundMe)

Autonomy
High

Biz Advantage
App-driven convenience, New economic models

Obstacle
Regulatory challenges, gig economy instability

Drivers for Change
- Market saturation
- Regulatory challenges
- Need for accelerated Innovation

In the 2010s, mobile phones became more affordable and accessible, quickly becoming a common sight in the hands of people everywhere. This widespread adoption of mobile technology was accompanied by high levels of autonomy, as awareness and expertise in building and leading platforms grew. However, market saturation also became a significant challenge, with many industries becoming overcrowded and highly competitive. Businesses faced evolving regulatory challenges, navigating increasingly complex legal landscapes. The failure to innovate became a critical issue, with companies unable to keep up with technological advancements and changing consumer preferences quickly falling behind more agile competitors. A notable example of success during this period is Apple Inc., which made a significant impact by creating a unique level of user experience with its products and platforms (more on this in the case study in Section D of the book). The key drivers leading into the next decade included the rise of cloud computing, the proliferation of sharing economy platforms, and the accelerating need for innovation.

In The 2020s

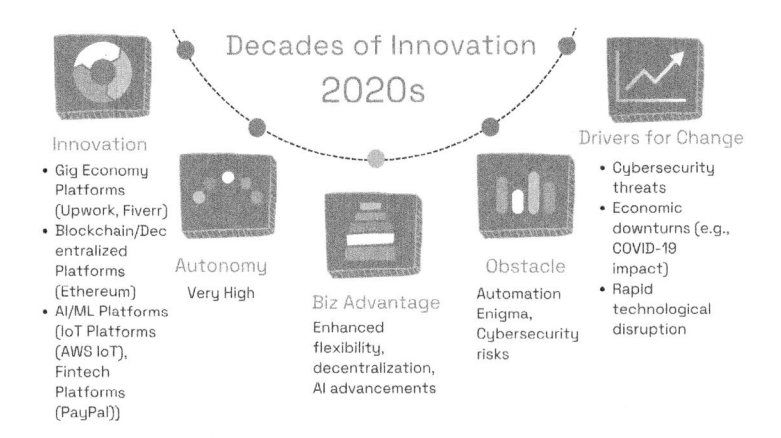

Decades of Innovation 2020s

Innovation
- Gig Economy Platforms (Upwork, Fiverr)
- Blockchain/Decentralized Platforms (Ethereum)
- AI/ML Platforms (IoT Platforms (AWS IoT), Fintech Platforms (PayPal))

Autonomy
Very High

Biz Advantage
Enhanced flexibility, decentralization, AI advancements

Obstacle
Automation Enigma, Cybersecurity risks

Drivers for Change
- Cybersecurity threats
- Economic downturns (e.g., COVID-19 impact)
- Rapid technological disruption

The **2020s**, although still ongoing, have already presented significant challenges for businesses. The COVID-19 pandemic led to severe economic downturns, impacting businesses across the globe. However, on the positive side, the pandemic also accelerated the opening of markets and drove businesses to reach very high levels of autonomy. People began building their businesses from anywhere, leading to a proliferation of innovative business models such as C2C (Consumer to Consumer), D2C (Direct to Consumer), H2H (Human to Human), and developer-centric models. These models have allowed individuals and organizations to adapt to new market realities quickly, fostering a culture of entrepreneurship and innovation that is more inclusive and accessible than ever before.

At the same time, cybersecurity threats have become more prevalent, with businesses needing to invest heavily in protecting their digital assets. Rapid technological disruption continues to shape the business landscape, with companies needing to adapt quickly to survive. Despite these challenges, the estimated failure rate has decreased, suggesting that businesses are becoming more resilient and better equipped to handle these evolving challenges.

This wave is also leading to increased spoken and written awareness on platform topics, serving as a correction wave to build true platforms and leverage them for greater business and economic value. The rise of these diverse business models is not just a reaction to current challenges but also a proactive strategy for future-proofing businesses against ongoing and unforeseen disruptions, with even more advancements to come in areas like AI/ML and emerging experiential technologies.

Platform Revolution: Insights from Decades of Innovation

1. **Shift from Hardware to Software to AI-driven platforms:** The focus of technological innovation has progressively shifted from hardware (1960s-70s) to software

(1980s-2000s) and now to AI-driven platforms (2020s). This progression reflects the growing importance of software and data in driving technological advancement and business models. Meanwhile, seamless hardware capabilities have grown tremendously, enabling advancements in software and AI/ML.

2. **Centralization to Decentralization:** The trend towards decentralization has transformed platforms, moving from centralized mainframe systems to decentralized blockchain and cloud-native platforms. While this enhances flexibility and resilience, it also brings challenges like cybersecurity threats, region-specific regulations etc.

3. **Increasing Autonomy and Complexity:** Platform technologies have evolved from low to very high autonomy, with early systems relying heavily on centralized control and modern platforms leveraging AI and decentralized systems. This shift has reduced the need for human intervention while increasing system complexity more and more granular components require integration and continuous change at the same time.

4. **Persistent Security and Regulatory Challenges:** Security vulnerabilities and regulatory compliance have been significant challenges since the 1980s. As platforms became more integrated into daily life, these issues have grown more complex, especially with the rise of AI and global data privacy regulations.

5. **Economic Influences on Technology:** Technological

evolution is closely tied to economic conditions, such as the dot-com bubble of the 2000s and the market shifts during the COVID-19 pandemic in the 2020s. These economic factors have significantly shaped the trajectory and success rates of platform technologies.

6. **Technological Infrastructure as a Limiting Factor:** The development and success of platforms have often been constrained by the existing technological infrastructure. Advancements in cloud computing and AI have expanded possibilities, but early limitations in infrastructure set the pace for platform adoption. Coming along with skill gaps to know about so many things and information at the same time. Which is not new however clearer at this stage.

7. **Need for Holistic Platform Awareness and Strategic Planning:** As platforms have grown in complexity, the need for specialized skills and forward-thinking strategic planning has become crucial. A holistic understanding and a well-defined blueprint are essential to efficiently leverage technology and ensure platform success in the long term.

As technological permutations multiply, the challenge of maintaining simplicity and scalability grows. This increasing complexity demands advanced management and integration skills. The evolution towards greater platform autonomy—where systems become more self-sufficient and less reliant on human intervention—highlights the ongoing need for continuous learning and adaptation in the face of rapid technological change.

These insights reveal the profound impact of globalization, open innovation, and technological advancements on platform evolution. They also emphasize the market's growing need for organizations to transform into platform companies—many of which have become some of the world's most valuable companies, driving continuous cycles of innovation.

As we conclude this chapter, I hope you've gained eye-opening perspectives on the complexities and opportunities within the platform landscape, enabling you to distinguish between genuine innovation and superficial trends.

Now, let's move forward to define what a true platform is and explore the framework that will guide you in leveraging these insights for success.

Key Takeaways

- The rapid evolution of platforms is driven by globalization, new business models, open innovation, and technological advancements, each contributing to both opportunities and challenges.

- The shift from centralized to decentralized systems and the increasing complexity of technologies have made platforms more autonomous but also introduced significant security and integration challenges.

- Understanding historical patterns in platform development is crucial for navigating modern challenges, enabling organizations to innovate effectively.

Chapter Three

Shattering Myths, Building Foundations

"A real platform earns its name through action, not just a title."

In previous chapters, we explored the vast opportunities platforms present and the immense innovation space they unlock. These platforms are becoming increasingly promising and essential for the future. While platforms are inherently composable by design, it's important to recognize that not every composition qualifies as a platform. Simply assembling components doesn't automatically create a platform—it requires much more than that.

Before we dive into the proper definitions and practical ways to leverage this space, it's crucial to dispel some prevailing myths.

Clarifying these misconceptions helps us focus on the real challenges and opportunities, ensuring that our efforts are directed toward what's genuinely relevant. These myths can sometimes distort our understanding, leading us away from the right solutions for our specific situations and organizations.

In this chapter, we'll address the question: 'What is not a platform?' Through practical examples, we'll highlight these myths, helping you better understand the distinctions and appreciate the nuances.

Let's begin by addressing these platform myths, setting a clear foundation for the journey ahead.

Platform vs. Myths - Let's begin

Myth 1: Platform vs. Portal

Misconception: Platforms and portals are interchangeable terms.

- *Reality:* While they may seem similar, platforms and portals serve different functions. A platform is a foundation that enables achieving broader goals and purposes with ease. A portal, on the other hand, is a user-facing interface or entry point that provides access to different services, resources, or applications, typically within a specific organization or environment. A portal focuses more on aggregation and presentation, while a platform provides the underlying structure and environment for development and deployment.

- *Acceptance:* Platforms may include portals as part of their service offering, but a platform's scope extends far beyond the portal's front-end experience.

- *Example:* Udemy serves as a portal where users—students and instructors—can access and interact with educational content, including courses, videos, and resources. However, Udemy's underlying platform enables instructors to create and upload courses, manage content, and interact with students. It also provides the tools and infrastructure to deliver content globally, process payments, and manage user data. The platform's scope extends beyond the portal's front end, facilitating the development, scaling, and maintenance of the entire learning ecosystem.

Myth 2: Platform vs. Framework

Misconception: Platforms and frameworks are interchangeable terms.

- ***Reality***: While they share similarities, platforms and frameworks serve different purposes in the software industry and software development. A platform provides a foundation for building and deploying applications, offering a broader range of functionalities and services, while a framework typically provides a set of pre-built tools, libraries, documents and other artefacts for developing specific types of applications within a defined structure or as per guidelines.

- ***Acceptance***: Platforms can be well-built using frameworks or blueprints, but they require significant effort from both providers and consumers.

- ***Example 1:*** The AWS Well-Architected Tool provides a framework to help architects design secure, efficient, and resilient infrastructures by offering best practices and recommendations. While it gives valuable guidance, the execution of improvements is left to the development teams. On the other hand, the Turbonomic Platform automates IT resource management, continuously analyzing and adjusting resources in real-time to maintain application performance, offering a more hands-off approach to optimization.

- ***Example 2:*** The NIST Cybersecurity Framework (NIST

CSF) provides guidelines to help organizations manage cybersecurity risks, focusing on five key areas: Identify, Protect, Detect, Respond, and Recover. It's widely used across industries to align cybersecurity efforts with business goals. Although I have not personally tested platforms like Palo Alto Networks Cortex XSOAR and IBM Security QRadar SOAR, they are widely regarded for their ability to automate threat detection and response by integrating security tools and automating tasks. These platforms enable security teams to efficiently manage incidents and improve overall security operations through automation.

Do you see the clear difference between a platform and a framework through the examples given above?

Myth 3: Platform vs. Platform Engineering

Misconception: Platform engineering is everything about any Platform.

- *Reality*: This misconception oversimplifies the role of platforms. Platform engineering is just one aspect of the broader platform journey. It is not the entirety of platform management; the complete journey involves much more. We will explore these aspects in greater detail in the upcoming chapters.

- *Acceptance*: Platform engineering helps streamline the development process, reduce complexity, and improve the overall efficiency of software delivery by providing a consistent and reliable system. This allows developers to focus on writing code rather than managing infrastructure. Platform engineering involves automating processes, ensuring scalability, and optimizing platform performance to make it user-friendly, maintainable, and efficient. It's similar to constructing the infrastructure and tools that support software applications, rather than creating the applications themselves or defining their purpose.

Myth 4: Platform (Engineering) vs. DevOps

Misconception: DevOps and platforms (engineering) is the same thing or more circulating questions are these the same thing?

- ***Reality:*** DevOps is a cultural and organizational approach that emphasizes collaboration, automation, and integration between development and operations teams to deliver software efficiently. Platform engineering builds on DevOps practices by addressing additional complexities such as on-demand infrastructure, continuous technology upgrades, and organization-specific processes, to simplify the platform development process. While DevOps focuses on software delivery, platform engineering requires continuous attention to manage the growing complexity at the platform development stage.

Myth 5: Platform vs. PaaS (Platform as a Service)

Misconception: Platforms and PaaS are synonymous.

- **Reality**: While PaaS is a type of platform business model, not all platforms are PaaS. PaaS typically refers to cloud computing services that provide a platform allowing customers to develop, run, and manage applications without managing the underlying infrastructure. Other types of platforms, such as IaaS (Infrastructure as a Service) and SaaS (Software as a Service), offer different levels of abstraction and functionality.

Myth 6: Platform vs. API (Application Programming Interface)

Misconception: Platforms and APIs are interchangeable terms.

- **Reality**: While APIs are a common component of platforms, they are not the same as platforms. An API is a set of rules and protocols that allows different software applications to communicate with each other. A platform, on the other hand, provides a comprehensive set of tools, services, and infrastructure for developing and deploying applications, which may include APIs as one of its components.

Myth 7: Platform vs. Operating System

Misconception: Platforms and operating systems serve the same purpose.

- **Reality**: An operating system manages hardware resources and provides services to applications, such as process management and file system access. This itself can be the type of platform and not everything about the platforms.

Myth 8: Platform vs. Containerization

Misconception: Platforms and containerization technologies like Docker, and Kubernetes are interchangeable.

- ***Reality***: Containerization is a technology concept that allows applications to be isolated and run in lightweight, portable containers, but platforms provide a broader range of services, including orchestration, scaling, and management of containerized applications.

Myth 9: Platform vs. Cloud Platforms

Misconception: Platforms and Cloud Platforms are interchangeable.

- **Reality**: "Cloud Platforms" is often a broad term used (or misused) to refer to major public cloud providers like AWS, GCP, and Azure. However, not everything these providers offer qualifies as a platform. While these cloud providers offer some services that function as platforms, it's important to distinguish between individual services and fully developed platforms.

Other Popular Myths

- Platforms must always expose UX/UI - In reality, not all

platforms need to have a user interface. Some platforms operate purely at the backend, providing services, APIs, or infrastructure without a direct user interface.

- **Add your list here**: This section can be used to identify and debunk additional misconceptions relevant to your organization or industry.

Breaking these myths is crucial to laying a solid foundation for our exploration. Sometimes, these misconceptions arise from a lack of awareness, while other times, they gain prominence due to overemphasis or marketing hype. Although these ideas are prevalent, they can obscure our understanding of platform patterns and principles if not addressed properly. That's why it was necessary to clarify these issues upfront. Now, as we move forward, it's worth reflecting on your own or your organization's context—are there tools or systems currently in use that are perceived as platforms? With these myths behind us, we can now delve into the specifics of Technology Platforms, aiming to decode their intricacies and set the stage for meaningful success.

Key Takeaways

- Not everything is a platform; many components are needed to build a truly useful and successful platform.

- If you have doubts about whether something qualifies as a platform or not, make a note now. Validate your understanding after reading the next chapter.

Chapter Four

Simplifying Platform Definition

"When it comes to technology platforms, it's important to have a clear vision to see it through."

In the previous chapter, we dispelled the myths surrounding technology platforms, laying the foundation for a clearer understanding. If you haven't read those chapters yet, I highly recommend doing so—they lay a strong foundation and simplify what might otherwise seem like a dense and overwhelming subject.

Now, it's time to establish a shared vocabulary. In this chapter, we'll start by defining 'Platform', followed by related terms such as 'Platform Economy', 'Platformization', and the roles and responsibilities within a platform ecosystem. These definitions will serve as foundation for our discussions throughout the book, helping us navigate the broader platform landscape with clarity. As we progress, our goal is to continue simplifying and connecting the essential knowledge about platforms starting with this chapter.

Technology Platforms Definition

Let's begin with the simplest way to remember what a true technology platform is before diving into a complete definition. To capture the essence of this concept, start by reading it from a platform user's perspective:

> **"If it elevates you with stability and clear integration, it's a platform; otherwise, it's just a fancy or in-progress technology."**

This serves as a concise and precise definition of technology platforms. However, to fully grasp the impact of this simplicity, it's important to explore why clear, straightforward definitions matter. Clear definitions make it easier to design, manage, and use technology effectively. Over-complicating these concepts often leads to misunderstandings, misaligned strategies, and, ultimately, the failure of platforms to deliver their intended value.

For readers interested in a more detailed, technical, or academic definition, and who wish to quickly gain a full perspective on technology platforms, here is a more comprehensive explanation:

> A technology platform is a comprehensive solution that provides complete functionality, whether it serves a single function or a set of functions. It is considered a complete platform from a technological perspective when it is stable (self-sufficient, adaptable, and repeatable) and easily integrates with other systems.
> - **Self-sufficient**: The platform can operate independently without constant intervention.
>
> - **Adaptable**: It can adjust to changes or scale as needed.
>
> - **Repeatable**: The processes and functions can be consistently replicated.
>
> - **Easily integrates**: The platform seamlessly connects with interfaces, external systems, tools, and technologies, enabling smooth interoperability and minimizing operational friction.
>
> This stability and ease of integration are key characteristics that distinguish a robust technology platform.

As you reflect on these definitions, I encourage you to think about the platforms you interact with or use in your day-to-day life—whether it's Netflix, LinkedIn, Google, or any other tech platform. What keeps you coming back to it? How does it integrate with your other systems? For example, how does Netflix sync with your smart TV, or how does Google link with your other devices? Engaging with these concepts personally can deepen your understanding and make the content more relevant to you.

The definition of a technology platform may seem simple, but it's grounded in extensive experience, research, and lessons learned from digital transformation projects. Many technology platforms start small as Minimum Viable Products (MVPs) and, over time, evolve into full-scale platforms. However, without careful planning, this evolution can result in isolated silos that require significant redesign to transform into cohesive platforms. This is where understanding platform fundamentals becomes critical.

If this resonates with you, feel free to give me a virtual high-five or share your thoughts in a review. If not, take a break, come back to this definition later, and reassess it within the context of your specific situation and business needs. This definition will likely become more relatable when viewed first from the perspective of a 'User' or 'Consumer', and then from the angles of platform integrator, provider, or even a critic.

In the upcoming sections, we'll explore numerous examples to continually test and validate these concepts. By grounding our approach in practical applications, we ensure the relevance of the definition, its connection to real-world platforms, and its ability to help readers achieve their platform goals.

Next, let's explore other commonly used terms in this book that will be helpful to understand as you continue reading.

Platformization

This trendy term underscores the significance of technology platforms, highlighting their widespread adaptation and acceptance across the global economy. It reflects how integral these platforms have become to modern business practices, daily life, and innovation.

Platform Economy

The platform economy represents a dynamic space where increasing portions of the economy are driven by the power of platforms. This influence affects both known and unknown players in the economy due to the widespread impact and usage of platforms, reshaping traditional business landscapes.

Key Roles in the Platform Economy

Various sources outline numerous roles and responsibilities within the platform economy, including platform users, consumers, partners, owners, providers, integrators, and more. However, as we delve deeper into this book, it's essential to focus specifically on technology platforms, emphasizing the most relevant aspects. This book will primarily concentrate on two crucial roles: Platform Providers and Platform Users. For further details on other roles and their distinctions, please refer to Appendix D, which includes an FAQ section.

Platform Providers

Entities responsible for designing, developing, and managing platforms. Their role is critical in ensuring platforms are not only equipped to meet immediate business needs but are also scalable, secure, user-friendly, and sustainable for future demands. The principles followed by providers help in creating adaptable platforms that evolve with varying business demands and technological advancements.

Platform Users

These are the entities or individuals responsible for selecting, implementing, and utilizing platforms. Their focus is on aligning platform capabilities with business goals and operational needs. The principles for platform users provide guidelines for effectively integrating platforms into existing systems and workflows, maximizing their utility and efficiency. Platform users differ from platform consumers, who are the end users leveraging the platform's final functionality (refer to Appendix F for examples). Platform users are more involved in enabling, leveraging, and enhancing the platform.

Network Effects

This occurs when a product or service becomes more valuable as more people use it. This phenomenon is a of platform economics, where the value of a platform increases as its user base grows. In other words, the more users a platform has, the more attractive it becomes to potential new users.

- **Direct Network Effects** – These effects arise when each new user directly adds value to the existing users. For example, with social media platforms like Facebook, the more people who join, the more connections, interactions, and content are available, making the platform more valuable for everyone involved.

- **Indirect Network Effects** – These effects occur when an increase in platform users attracts more complementary goods or services, which in turn enhances the platform's value. For example, as more people use a gaming console like PlayStation, more developers are incentivized to create games for it, which then makes the console more attractive to new users.

Connecting Concepts to Examples

Here are a couple of examples to help clarify the concepts covered in the earlier sections:

Example 1: Amazon serves as an e-commerce platform for both platform consumers—those who order items and platform users—those who integrate their products through Amazon. Does it elevate their purpose of selling or purchasing with stability? Can they rely on its various interfaces and integrations? If the answer is yes, then it qualifies as a technology platform (which, of course, it does, and that's why it's so popular). Amazon essentially encapsulates and automates many complex processes behind the scenes, providing stability through self-sufficiency, adaptability, and repeatability.

To further clarify, when we talk about platform providers, think of Amazon as the entity (platform provider) that designs, develops, and manages its e-commerce platform. Platform users are the businesses that integrate their products into Amazon's platform, utilizing its infrastructure to reach customers. Meanwhile, platform consumers are the end users—shoppers like you and me—who buy products from Amazon. This is illustrated in the diagram below:

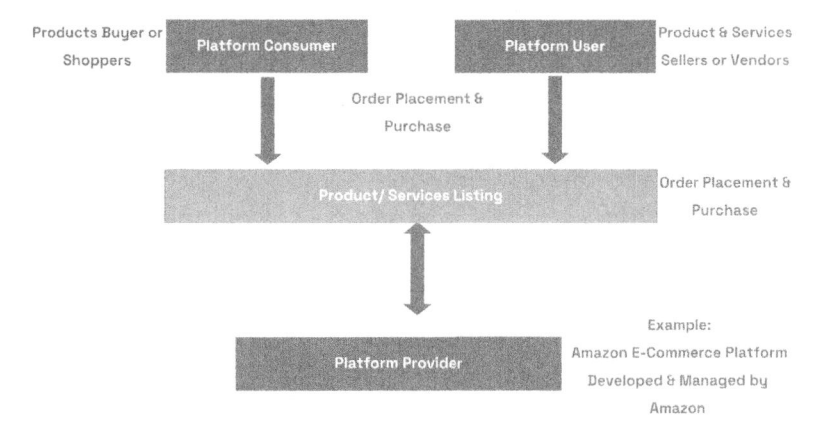

```
Products Buyer or          ┌─────────────────┐              ┌─────────────┐    Product & Services
Shoppers                   │ Platform Consumer│              │Platform User│    Sellers or Vendors
                           └────────┬────────┘              └──────┬──────┘
                                    │       Order Placement &      │
                                    │            Purchase          │
                                    ▼                              ▼
                           ┌──────────────────────────────────────────┐    Order Placement &
                           │         Product/ Services Listing        │         Purchase
                           └────────────────────┬─────────────────────┘
                                                ▲
                                                ▼
                                                                            Example:
                           ┌──────────────────────────┐                Amazon E-Commerce Platform
                           │    Platform Provider     │                Developed & Managed by
                           └──────────────────────────┘                        Amazon
```

Example 2: LinkedIn functions as a professional networking platform for both platform consumers—individuals who use the platform to connect with others, search for jobs, or showcase their professional profiles—and platform users—businesses or recruiters who use LinkedIn's tools to post job openings, promote their brand, or identify talent.

Does LinkedIn help these users achieve their goals of networking, hiring, or branding with stability and efficiency? Can they rely on LinkedIn's various features, such as messaging, job posting, and integration with third-party tools like applicant tracking systems? If the answer is yes, then LinkedIn qualifies as a technology platform. LinkedIn automates and streamlines many complex processes—such as job matching and profile recommendations—providing stability through its self-sufficient, adaptable, and repeatable systems.

To further clarify, when we talk about platform providers, think of LinkedIn as the entity that designs, develops, and manages its professional networking platform. Platform users are the businesses, recruiters, or companies that utilize LinkedIn's services, infrastructure to connect with potential employees or partners. Meanwhile, platform consumers are the end users—professionals like you and me—who use the platform to network, search for jobs, or engage with content.

In Summary

The examples above highlight the practical relevance of the foundational definitions we've discussed. These definitions will serve as the building blocks for the discussions and strategies that follow. As we progress through the subsequent chapters, these concepts will be revisited and expanded upon with deeper examples, helping you navigate the intricate world of technology platforms with greater confidence and clarity.

As we wrap up this chapter, take a moment to reflect on the definitions we've explored. The roles of platform providers, users, and consumers are central to the platform economy, and understanding these distinctions is key to leveraging platforms effectively. With these definitions in hand, you are now better equipped to engage with the platform strategies and principles that will be covered in the chapters ahead.

This concludes Section A. With a clearer understanding, let's move on to Section B, which offers universal insights and a blueprint relevant to all readers and technology platform types, regardless of their specific roles or the principles they follow. In contrast, Section C will dive deeper into the principles and patterns specific to platform providers.

With the foundational alignment in place, let's jump into the main course.

Key Takeaways

- Platform definitions can be simple yet comprehensive. It is crucial to distinguish between true platforms and platform-like entities to avoid confusion and misapplication.

- The platform ecosystem includes various participants. However, focusing on key roles, such as platform providers, users, and consumers, simplifies the process of developing and effectively using platforms.

- Understanding distinct roles and principles in the platform ecosystem helps create platforms that are not only functional but also sustainable and user-centric.

Section B

Universal Platform Success Patterns

Chapter Five

Platform Success Blueprint

"Platform paths are unwritten and tangled; an innovative blueprint is needed to weave them into success."

At this point, we have aligned on the key platform challenges, the surge of innovation, and the complexities organizations face when using or developing platforms. These organizations range from individual-driven platforms to large-scale enterprise solutions. We've also demystified common myths about platforms. Now, it's time to shift our focus to the solution space. If you haven't read the foundational chapters, I strongly recommend doing so. Without this background, conflicting views may arise, making it difficult to fully grasp and benefit from the Platform Success Blueprint.

Through extensive research on this topic, it's evident that managing these complexities is possible, and there is much to learn from successful platform companies. The key is to clearly identify the underlying problem in your context and then shift your perspective from the problem space to the platform and innovation space. The more you apply this approach to larger groups and impact areas, the more significant the learning and value that go into the platform. This approach holds the pieces to the puzzle.

Let's dive into how this framework can help manage and simplify these challenges.

Research shows that humans understand three-dimensional spaces best, which is why I've developed this mental model for you. Picture it as a cube, with each of its six sides representing a different aspect of platform complexities.

Building Our Vocabulary

We will adopt the specific terminology of a cube for consistency:

- **Cube**: The entire structure represents the comprehensive view of the platform.

- **Sides**: The large, flat surfaces of the cube, referred to as sides (or faces), represent the six key dimensions of the platform. Each side will be addressed individually, focusing on a different and essential aspect of the platform, one at a time.

- **Cubies or Cublets**: The smaller cubes that make up the cube, representing the individual components or modules within each dimension of the platform.

- **Layers**: The cube can be visualized as being solved layer by layer, with each layer consisting of a 3x3 grid of cubies. These layers represent the stages or levels of platform maturity and development.

Understanding these terms will help when describing specific parts of the platform framework as we move forward.

Introduction – Six Sides of Platform Blueprint

Now that we've established the terminology, let's dive into the six faces of the platform framework. This model is designed to encapsulate all critical aspects of a technology platform. By detailing six distinct faces (or sides), it provides a holistic perspective that ensures no element—from strategy to design, development, and continuous innovation—is overlooked. Each face represents a crucial dimension, enabling stakeholders to systematically address every aspect, from architecture and scalability to security and user experience.

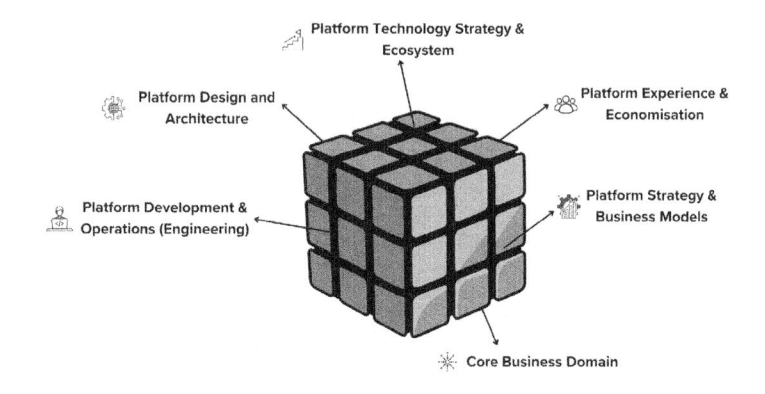

Platform Technology Strategy & Ecosystem

Platform Design and Architecture

Platform Experience & Economisation

Platform Development & Operations (Engineering)

Platform Strategy & Business Models

Core Business Domain

The significance of this framework lies in its comprehensive approach to managing complex platform ecosystems. It serves as a strategic tool, guiding businesses in innovating and optimizing their platforms effectively, and facilitating better decision-making and planning. By covering the entire scope of a technology platform, this framework not only supports current development practices but also anticipates future needs and challenges, ensuring that the platform remains robust, scalable, and competitive in an ever-evolving digital landscape.

Once this simplicity is mastered for a single platform, the same blueprint can be extrapolated to manage a platform of platforms or multiple interconnected platforms. This expanded application allows organizations to seamlessly integrate various platforms, maximizing efficiency and fostering innovation across the entire digital ecosystem. Leveraging this comprehensive framework ensures coherence and synergy among platforms, driving sustained growth and adaptability in today's dynamic technology landscape.

This blueprint is composed of the following six sides, each covering a vital aspect of a technology platform:

1. Core Business Domain

2. Platform Strategy & Business Models

3. Platform Experience & Economization

4. Platform Technology Strategy & Ecosystem

5. Platform Design and Architecture

6. Platform Development To Operations (Includes Platform Engineering)

This platform blueprint is a complete model designed to encapsulate all critical aspects of a technology platform. By detailing six distinct sides, it provides a holistic view that ensures no element of platform strategy to development and management is overlooked. Each side represents a crucial dimension, allowing stakeholders to systematically address every aspect, from architecture and scalability to security and user experience.

Core Business Domain

The core business domain refers to the fundamental areas of operations and value creation that the platform is designed to support and optimize. This typically includes the main products or services that a platform company provides or integrates with to serve end customers and users. For example, in an e-commerce platform like Amazon, the core business domain includes online retail, logistics, payment processing, and customer service. In the automotive industry, companies like BMW and Ford focus on providing vehicles, parts, accessories, and related services through platforms that serve customers in various ways.

This domain also involves the strategic management of data and interactions between users and service providers, ensuring reliability, scalability, and security. For instance, in a digital banking platform, services like online banking, mobile transactions, and loan processing are part of the core business domain, with a focus on managing sensitive financial data securely.

Focusing on its core business domain allows a technology platform to align with business needs, streamline operations, enhance user experience, and build a robust ecosystem that attracts and retains users. This side of the blueprint is discussed in more detail in Chapter 6.

Platform Strategy & Business Models

Platform strategy and business models focus on how a platform creates, delivers, or captures value within its ecosystem. This involves defining the target audience, understanding their needs, and developing a value proposition that attracts and retains users. Effective platform strategies leverage network effects wherever possible in conjunction with the business models. For example, Airbnb connects hosts with guests, charging service fees to ensure profitability while scaling the platform. Another example could be Samsung leveraging the Android platform through its Galaxy Store, offering exclusive apps and services that enhance user experience and drive customer retention while sharing revenue with developers.

This side of the blueprint is discussed in more detail in Chapter 7.

Platform Experience and Economization

Platform experience and Economization refer to the interface and interactions exposed to both internal and external customers, focusing on optimizing operational efficiency and financial performance. This concept encompasses the user experience of individuals involved with the platform and the careful Economization of resources to ensure cost-effective and realistic platform operation. Strategic investments in technology, user experience, and brand building are also key elements, all while maintaining sustainability. For example, Amazon achieves this by leveraging advanced logistics, data analytics, and cloud computing to offer competitive prices while maintaining profitability and a high-quality user experience.

This side of the blueprint is discussed in more detail in Chapter 8.

Platform Technology Strategy and Ecosystem

The platform technology strategy and ecosystem development are crucial for the success of technology-driven platforms. This aspect of the platform is often the most focused on, yet it can become overcrowded with insufficient practical planning. It involves making strategic technology decisions, planning for operational requirements, and ensuring the right level of involvement and contribution to the broader technology ecosystem. For example, Apple's iOS platform thrives due to its strategic control over hardware and software integration, creating a cohesive technology ecosystem that benefits both developers and users, fostering innovation and consistency.

This side of the blueprint is discussed in more detail in Chapter 9.

Platform Design and Architecture

Platform design and architecture focus on the technical aspects of the platform, emphasizing alignment with the overall technology strategy. This involves selecting appropriate technologies, ensuring the platform supports seamless integration with other systems, and prioritizing both functional and non-functional growth. The design must account for infrastructure, networking, and the scalability needed to handle future demands. Additionally, it should facilitate integration and interoperability with internal and external systems, ensuring the platform remains versatile and adaptable.

This side of the blueprint is discussed in more detail in Chapter 10.

Platform Development and Operations

Platform development, often referred to as engineering, involves the technical development and ongoing enhancement of the platform. This includes designing and constructing the core infrastructure while ensuring scalability, reliability, and security. Platform engineers focus on integrating new features, optimizing performance, and maintaining the platform's ability to handle increasing loads. This phase builds upon the design and architecture established for the platform. The development process is iterative, incorporating constant feedback and updates to refine development practices. For instance, the development of Microsoft Azure involved creating a robust cloud infrastructure that supports a wide range of services, from computing to storage, enabling businesses to efficiently build and deploy applications.

This side of the blueprint is discussed in more detail in Chapter 11.

Common Aspects of Platform Success Blueprint

In addition to these six dimensions, two more critical aspects will be explored: the platform journey for users and providers, covered in Chapters 12 and 13, respectively.

- Platform Technology Strategy & Ecosystem
- Platform Design and Architecture
- Platform Experience & Economisation
- Platform Development (Engineering)
- Platform Strategy & Business Models
- Layers of Maturity & Composition
- Core Business Domain

Security | Measurement | Innovation

Platform Providers - Continuous Process

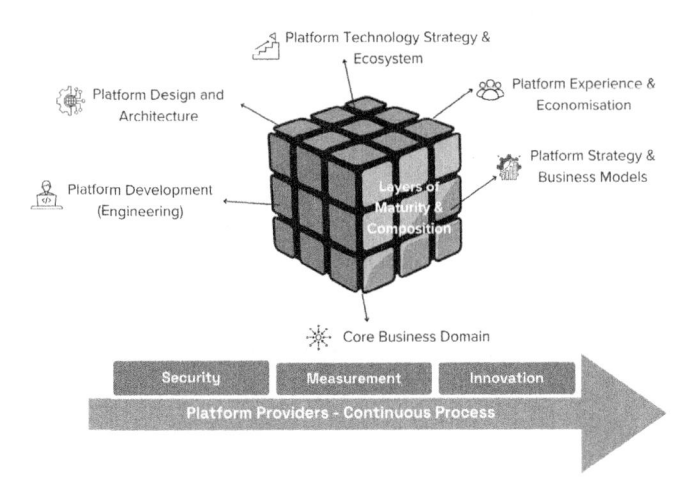

Moreover, certain elements apply universally across all sides of the platform and are not repeated in each chapter but addressed wherever relevant. These include security, innovation, and metrics. Both users and providers should consistently keep these aspects in mind throughout the platform journey, as they apply to each side of the blueprint that we will read.

Based on these explanations, you can now deep dive into the relevant faces of the Platform Success Blueprint that best suits your needs. The following table helps you understand and relate each aspect to your context.

Blueprint Face	Purpose and Relevancy	Refer
Core Business Domain	Absolutely necessary for all types of platforms	Chapter 6
Platform Strategy and Business Models	Important for all platforms and for both platform users and providers	Chapter 7
Platform Experience and Economisation	Important for all platforms and for both platform users and providers	Chapter 8
Platform Technology Strategy & Ecosystem	Important for all platform providers (and users in some cases)	Chapter 9
Platform Design and Architecture	Important for all platforms providers (and users in some cases)	Chapter 10
Platform Development and Operations	Important for all platforms providers (and users in some cases)	Chapter 11
Platform Journey for Users	Important for all platform users	Chapter 12
Platform Journey for Providers	Important for all platform providers	Chapter 13

Effective Usage of the Platform Blueprint

The following table helps you understand and relate each aspect to your context:

Let's delve into these six essential aspects of any platform, followed by an exploration of the platform journey for both users and providers. This journey culminates in a comprehensive case study to deepen your understanding. Join me as we navigate the intricate world of platform technology, guided by this framework. Together, we'll uncover the crucial elements that drive successful platform businesses and explore the strategies that make them thrive.

Key Takeaways

- The Platform Success Blueprint is a comprehensive model that covers every crucial aspect of platform strategy, development, and management, ensuring no element is overlooked.

- Security, innovation, and metrics apply universally across all aspects of the platform blueprint, requiring continuous attention throughout the platform journey.

- While the principles for platform users and providers are the same, their journeys differ in complexity and steps.

Chapter Six

Connect The Core Business Domain

"Think of platforms as canvases; without a core business, they remain blank - lacking purpose and direction."

In today's world, core businesses and platforms are deeply intertwined. Your core business often requires a robust platform—or multiple platforms (serving as your canvas)—to effectively reach and satisfy your audience. Conversely, a powerful platform needs a strong core business to fulfil its purpose and achieve sustained success.

The core business domain is the bread and butter that a platform company offers to its customers and users. The term 'domain' refers to the specific area of expertise and central business focus that defines the company's operations. The core business domain of a technology platform encompasses the fundamental areas of operations and value creation that the platform is designed to support and optimize. For large companies, this can extend beyond the platform itself, while for small to medium-sized companies, it may be entirely platform-centric, or involve various combinations in between.

The domain encompasses the key functions and services that drive the platform's economic and operational success. For example, in an e-commerce platform like Amazon, the core business domain includes the entire online retail ecosystem, encompassing logistics, payment processing, suppliers, packaging, and customer service. Each of these areas is critical for the platform's overall performance and customer satisfaction. We will explore more examples shortly.

If the platform itself is your business, it is essential to understand all aspects of this cube. If you're building your business using a combination of platform technologies, this foundation represents the core of your operations. While this book does not delve into the specifics of business domains—a vast area beyond its scope, varying widely from one business to another—it does emphasize the importance of understanding how core domain teams are influenced by and interact with the platform. This interaction directly or indirectly impacts their workflows and overall effectiveness.

Let's start by exploring a few example domains and the services they offer through platforms. This will help you relate these concepts to your context by showing how they apply in different scenarios. Afterwards, we'll dive into the key success factors needed to thrive in these business domains through effective platform strategy.

Example 1: Online Education Platform Business Model and Services

Online education platforms like Udemy and Coursera bridge the gap between educators and learners by offering a diverse array of courses across multiple disciplines.

Business Functions/ Services:

- **Course Marketplace:** A platform where instructors create and sell courses, while learners browse and purchase them.

- **Learning Management System (LMS):** A suite of tools for course creation, content management, and student assessment, providing a seamless learning experience.

- **Certification Programs:** Accredited courses and specializations that award learners certifications upon completion, enhancing their credentials.

- **Corporate Training Solutions:** Tailored training programs for businesses, often including tracking and reporting features to monitor progress.

- **Community and Support:** Forums, discussion boards, and support services to facilitate interaction between learners and instructors.

Example 2: Cloud Provider Business Model and Services

Cloud platform providers like AWS, Google Cloud, and Microsoft Azure offer a comprehensive suite of services that empower businesses to undergo digital transformation and scale efficiently.

Business Functions/ Services:

- **Infrastructure as a Service (IaaS):** Provides virtualized computing resources over the internet, enabling businesses to rent virtual machines, storage, and networking components as needed.

- **Platform as a Service (PaaS):** A development environment for building, testing, and deploying applications without managing the underlying infrastructure.

- **Software as a Service (SaaS):** Delivers software applications over the Internet on a subscription basis, eliminating the need for internal hosting.

- **Data Analytics and Machine Learning:** Provides tools and frameworks for analyzing large datasets and building machine learning models for actionable insights.

- **Security and Compliance:** Offers comprehensive security measures, including encryption, identity management, and compliance certifications, to ensure data protection and regulatory adherence.

Example 3: Media and Entertainment Platform Business Model and Services

Media and entertainment platforms like Netflix, Spotify, and YouTube leverage digital technology to deliver content to a global audience.

Business Functions/ Services:

- **Content Streaming:** Delivers video, music, and other media content over the internet, available on-demand for consumers.

- **Subscription Services:** Offers tiered subscription plans with varying levels of access to content, often including ad-free options.

- **Content Creation and Distribution:** Provides tools and services for creators to produce, upload, and distribute their content widely.

- **Personalization and Recommendations:** Uses algorithms that analyze user behaviour to recommend tailored content, enhancing engagement.

- **Monetization Options:** Provides various revenue streams for content creators, including ad revenue, pay-per-view, and premium subscriptions.

Example 4: Digital Bank's Core Business and Services

Digital banks offer essential services such as deposits, withdrawals, loans, and investments while ensuring regulatory compliance through specialized risk management.

Business Functions/ Services:

- **Digital Banking Platforms:** Integrates online banking services with traditional banking.

- **Mobile Banking Apps:** Provides real-time transaction processing and convenient mobile access.

- **Risk Management Platforms:** Offers specialized risk assessment and management processes to maintain stability and compliance.

Example 5: Hybrid Telecom Platform Business Model and Services

A Hybrid Telecom platform connects telecom service providers with consumers seeking customized solutions, facilitating service selection, subscriptions, billing, and communication.

Business Functions/ Services:

- **Network Provisioning:** Manages setup and activation of services, ensuring quick and reliable delivery.

- **Mobile Networks:** Optimizes 4G and 5G operations for high-speed connectivity.

- **Fiber Optic Networks:** Oversees deployment and maintenance of high-speed internet services.

- **Network Management:** Monitors and manages network performance.

- **Billing and Payment Processing:** Provides systems for accurate billing and efficient payments.

- **Customer Support:** Delivers comprehensive support, including 24/7 technical assistance.

- **User Interface:** Provides a user-friendly website and app for efficient service management.

- **Network Interoperability:** Ensures compatibility between various services and devices for a seamless user experience.

These distinct business domains and services illustrate how digital technology platforms are leveraged across various sectors to enhance efficiency, improve accessibility, and increase user engagement. While this list could be extended, it's crucial to observe how complexity increases with each successive example. If you didn't notice this on your first read, I encourage you to revisit the examples, taking your time to fully grasp the scale and hybrid complexities involved, whether in infrastructure, product range, or business models.

One striking aspect of these examples is that many of the sub-services within each domain either offer or develop platforms themselves. Let's explore this further.

Core Business and Platforms Integration

The biggest challenges arise when platform teams fail to adequately prepare the business for upcoming changes or the integration of platforms[1]. Here are some examples from my experience that could be invaluable in guiding you toward platform success:

Leadership and Strategic Planning

Platforms often falter when platform leadership neglects to emphasize strategy, vision, transparency, and translating platform benefits to the business—who also serve as the primary customers for platform teams. In nearly all instances where platforms struggled to succeed, the primary reason was a lack of strategic planning and adoption of platform knowledge by businesses. Platform leaders often find themselves deeply immersed in the technical aspects of their teams, while neglecting crucial aspects like business buy-in, preparedness, and learning. This is reminiscent of a common product development pitfall: 'Never build a product that doesn't solve a problem.' Those with product development experience will undoubtedly resonate with this principle.

Another critical oversight occurs when the economics of the platform and its business impact are not communicated to the business. The dynamic and varying nature of costing models today often leads to confusion. Additionally, there's the challenge of ecosystem development, which involves fostering a vibrant network of developers, partners, and users around the platform. This ecosystem directly influences the value delivered through platform adoption and significantly impacts overall performance and scalability.

Platform leaders need to embrace platform thinking and ensure it infuses throughout the organization.

Business Team's Platform Understanding and Nurturing

The success of platform development and adoption heavily depends on how well teams are prepared and guided toward a platform-oriented mindset. It is vital to train teams thoroughly, keep them well-informed, and provide clear visibility into platform roadmaps. Equally important is building a community that fosters ongoing learning about the platform, driving both loyalty and engagement. Additionally, it's crucial to prepare teams for change, ensuring they can confidently navigate new processes and technologies as the platform evolves.

Platform Integration and Adoption at the Business Level

Successful platform integration and adoption often require technical involvement and development. From my experience, aligning three key areas is critical to determining the success of a business integration:

1. **Interoperability Standards**: Clearly defining and understanding interoperability standards is essential. Success is more likely when there's a comprehensive grasp of how different infrastructures, compute resources, services, or platform interfaces interact. This foresight supports the seamless transition to new ways of working and ensures the platform's continuous evolution.

2. **Encapsulating Platform Changes**: A highly effective approach is through a robust API ecosystem (or similar frameworks) and management. Developing and managing APIs enables third-party integrations and enhances platform functionality. This approach allows external developers to build on the platform without needing to understand the underlying changes, driving adoption and value. Similarly, internal business teams can also be shielded from platform complexities.

3. **Continuous Innovation and Feature Development**: Maintaining continuous innovation and feature development is vital for keeping the platform relevant. Ensuring visibility, seeking early feedback, and planning for growth keep the platform aligned with evolving business needs.

Platform success is not a one-time achievement but a continuous process of iteration and improvement. Establishing robust feedback loops between the platform team and the business is crucial for adapting to changing needs and ensuring long-term success. Regular feedback from internal teams and external users helps platform providers identify pain points, discover new opportunities, and make informed decisions about feature development. This ongoing dialogue ensures the platform evolves in line with business objectives and user expectations, ultimately leading to higher adoption rates and stronger user engagement. Adopting an agile approach, where feedback is integrated into every stage of platform development, significantly enhances the platform's ability to remain relevant and competitive in a rapidly changing digital landscape. We'll explore how this integrates holistically in Section D, but first, let's examine all the necessary aspects.

As we explore integration, it's important to consider how the platform experience influences adoption at different levels within the business, ensuring that both user satisfaction and operational efficiency are aligned.

Platform Experience

While the previous points are crucial, platform experience remains the cornerstone of successful platform adoption and retention. Delivering value directly through the platform is key. For example, ensure onboarding, user interaction, and learning are intuitive and seamless, minimizing the need for manual intervention. This approach not only reduces operational and customer support burdens but also enhances user satisfaction.

When complemented by effective content management, active user engagement, and robust feedback mechanisms, this strategy can address and overcome most challenges, leading to a successful platform within the business. We will explore this further in the upcoming case study, after covering the essential pillars of the Platform Success Blueprint.

Focusing on these three areas can significantly enhance the likelihood of successful platform integration and adoption, ensuring both technical and operational alignment. While the primary responsibility should lie with the platform teams, cooperation and adaptability from business leaders are crucial for creating a win-win scenario for the organization.

The success of a platform strategy is directly tied to how well-defined your organization's business strategy is. A clear business strategy enables your platform to scale, connect with and leverage the ecosystem, and attract both producers and consumers. Ensuring that platform teams lead the initiative while business leaders provide support and adaptability lays a strong foundation for growth and innovation.

Checklist for Core Business Integration

The checklist below can be revisited regularly. Prioritize one platform at a time based on its importance to your business, and evaluate it against your specific scenario to establish a solid platform strategy and implementation roadmap. This checklist highlights essential elements for effective integration and engagement with core business domain teams, whether they are technical or non-technical communities. Feel free to extend and customize it according to your needs.

Leadership and Strategic Planning

- Do you understand the economic model of platforms, including network effects and economies of scale, and how these factors impact your business?

- How do you define and communicate the unique value proposition that your platform offers to both internal and external customers?

- Have you developed monetization strategies such as subscription models, transaction fees, or advertising? How effective have these strategies been?

- What cost management strategies have you implemented to optimize operational expenses, and are they yielding the desired results?

- How do you foster the growth of a vibrant ecosystem of

developers, partners, and users around your platform?

- Are you utilizing business analytics to extract insights from platform data to inform decision-making? How successful has this approach been?

- How do you ensure that the platform's vision and mission align with the broader business strategy and goals?

Platform Experience

- Have you developed efficient and user-friendly onboarding processes for new platform users? Are they proving successful?

- What are your primary focus areas in user experience design to ensure the platform is intuitive and user-friendly?

- How do you maintain a content management strategy to keep platform content relevant and up-to-date?

- What tactics do you employ to increase user engagement and activity on the platform? Have these tactics been effective?

- How do you create channels for collecting and acting on user feedback to drive continuous platform improvement?

- What infrastructure have you developed to handle customer support inquiries and issues effectively? How well does it perform?

Platform Integration and Business-Level Adoption

- Do you have a scalability plan to accommodate growth in users, transactions, and data volume?

- How do you efficiently allocate resources to support platform development and operations?

- How do you ensure your platform meets all relevant regulatory and compliance requirements? Have you encountered any challenges?

- How do you build and manage partnerships with other companies to enhance platform capabilities? Can you share any success stories?

- What processes have you developed for resolving conflicts between platform users and partners? How effective are these processes?

Business Teams' Platform Understanding, Nurturing, and Education

- What training programs do you implement to ensure internal teams and users can effectively use the platform?

- How do you prepare for change management to handle transitions and updates smoothly?

- How do you build and nurture a loyal, engaged community around the platform?

As you reflect on these strategies and insights, consider how they apply to your own organization's platform journey. By tailoring these principles to your specific context, you can build a robust platform that not only aligns with your core business objectives but also drives long-term success. In the next chapter, we will delve deeper into the practical applications of these strategies, exploring real-world case studies and actionable steps to further enhance your platform's impact.

Key Takeaways

- Ensure your platforms align with and actively support core business objectives to drive sustained success.

- Core business requirements should be fully integrated and reflected in the platform roadmap and strategy.

- Proactively educate and engage business teams in platform knowledge.

- Continuously assess how effectively your platform integrates with the business.

---

1. https://www.hfsresearch.com/research/your-cloud-transformation-will-fail-if-it-is-not-grounded-in-business-objectives/

Chapter Seven

Crafting Platform Strategy

"Hope and progress are not Platform strategy."

Let's begin this chapter by breaking the pattern to make new patterns

Do you know platforms have 5 times more failures than successes?[1] Let's look at some popular failures and their root causes.

Example 1: Misalignment with Core Business Functions

- **Company:** eBay

- **Misstep:** In the early 2000s, eBay attempted to diversify its business by acquiring companies such as Skype and StumbleUpon. These acquisitions were not well-aligned with eBay's core business of online auctions and e-commerce.

- **Impact:** These misalignments led to inefficiencies and distracted eBay from focusing on its main marketplace, ultimately resulting in divestments.

> "I felt that focus was a really important element in the Internet today and in our company. You can't compete and succeed on multiple fronts." - eBay CEO[2]

Example 2: Inadequate Experience and Economization

- **Company:** MySpace

DECODING PLATFORM PATTERNS

- **Misstep**: **MySpace** (a company born in 2003) failed to evolve its platform based on user feedback and changing preferences, especially in areas such as user interface design and privacy controls.

- **Impact**: As a result, users migrated to Facebook, which continuously innovated based on user feedback and needs, leading to MySpace's significant decline in popularity and user base.

> "Every time we tried to professionalize the place they resisted." - Ross Levinsohn, MySpace Executive[3]

Example 3: Failure to Build an Ecosystem

- **Company:** GE Predix (Cloud Platform)

- **Misstep**: GE's Predix platform struggled with the "chicken-or-egg" problem, failing to attract enough third-party developers to create a robust ecosystem outside of GE's customers.

- **Impact**: Predix's limited adoption and ecosystem growth led to the platform's decline, marking a significant setback in GE's digital transformation efforts.

"GE said they expected Predix software to do for factories and plants what Apple's iOS did for cell phones."[4]

Example 4: Poor Integration with Technology & Ecosystem

- **Company:** BlackBerry

- **Misstep**: BlackBerry failed to effectively integrate its platform with the broader app ecosystem. Its proprietary operating system and limited app store offerings could not compete with iOS and Android.

- **Impact**: As a result, BlackBerry lost significant market share to competitors who provided better app integration and a more comprehensive technology ecosystem, leading to a drastic decline in its smartphone business.

"Forget about today's market. The more important thing is what do you believe that the market beyond looks like." - John Chen, Blackberry CEO[5]

Example 5: Overlooking Security and Compliance

- **Company:** Microsoft Azure

- **Misstep**: In 2021, a significant vulnerability in Azure's Cosmos DB, called "ChaosDB," was discovered, allowing potential attackers to access databases of multiple clients without authorization. The flaw arose from a misconfiguration in a data visualization feature, impacting several high-profile customers.

- **Impact**: Microsoft Azure's vulnerability underscored the significant risks associated with cloud services, raising concerns among enterprise clients about the security of their data. Each time such incidents occur, they shake customers' confidence and dampen their appetite for adopting new technologies.

Example 6: Lack of Scalability and Flexibility

- **Company:** Friendster

- **Misstep**: Friendster's platform was not designed to scale efficiently, which led to significant performance issues as the user base grew.

- **Impact**: Users experienced slow load times and frequent outages, prompting many to switch to other social networks like Facebook and MySpace. Friendster's inability to scale effectively contributed to its failure.[6]

Example 7: Inability to Compete with Established Players

- **Company:** Microsoft Mixer

- **Misstep**: Mixer, Microsoft's streaming platform, failed to gain a significant user base despite heavy investment, including the acquisition of top streamers.

- **Impact**: Mixer was shut down in 2020, with Microsoft redirecting users to Facebook Gaming, unable to compete with Twitch and YouTube Gaming.

> "We started pretty behind, in terms of where Mixer's monthly active viewers were compared to some of the big players out there," - Phil Spencer, Microsoft's head of gaming[7]

The examples shared above offer valuable lessons that anyone can leverage. By examining the successes and failures of platform companies, we uncover essential insights for building resilient and thriving platforms. These stories highlight the importance of aligning platform strategy with core business objectives, effectively engaging users, prioritizing security, ensuring scalability, and seamlessly integrating with the broader digital ecosystem—in other words, creating network effects.

Platforms often fail at an alarming rate due to issues like poor scalability and misaligned strategies. However, by identifying and understanding these common areas of failures, platform teams can make informed decisions that not only avoid these mistakes but also drive sustained growth and user engagement.

With these insights in mind, let's delve into the fundamental elements that contribute to platform success and how they can be strategically implemented.

Leading with Platform Strategy

The Platform Functions

Functions of your platform, derived directly from your core business domain, are central to your platform blueprint. The guiding principle is clear - focus on what you do best, your core competencies and ensure that your platform supports and enhances these functions before expanding into parallel areas. These platform functions define what your technology must facilitate, encompassing everything from operational processes and customer interactions to value-creation activities. By identifying and aligning these functions, you ensure that every aspect of your technology infrastructure is strategically geared towards achieving your business goals.

Choosing and nurturing platform functions involves making deliberate decisions about which business processes to elevate through platform technology. For example, Tesla has strategically integrated functions like autonomous driving and over-the-air software updates into their platform, leveraging advanced AI and software development to align with their core business. Similarly, Google's acquisition of Android and Facebook's acquisition of Instagram illustrates how selecting the right platform functions can drive innovation and maintain a competitive edge.

Equally, it's crucial to recognize that simply adopting a platform approach won't revive a struggling product on its own. A successful platform strategy requires clarity—knowing both what to do and, just as importantly, what not to do. This clarity in defining platform functions is critical, as it directly impacts the platform's success and sustainability.

Always maintain a prioritized list of platform functions. Don't allow undesirable elements to creep in just to fill gaps or maintain momentum.

Platform Business Model

Ideally, the business model is selected well before the platform strategy is defined. However, there are cases where the platform comes first, and its business impact, consumers, and users align over time. For example, large-scale expansion may require the creation of platform network effects, which can involve opening the platform to developers or other ecosystem partners as it evolves.

In any case, understanding and selecting the right business model is a crucial step in shaping your platform strategy. Not all business models align equally well with the platform economy, so it's essential to assess and integrate those that best support your objectives. By doing so, you can leverage the platform's success blueprint to enhance operations and realize significant benefits. While the Platform Business Model was discussed in detail in Chapter 2, more insights can be found in Appendix B, which offers key guidance on selecting the models best suited to your specific platform context.

The landscape of business models and technology is ever-evolving. Who would have predicted in the early 2000s that Human-to-Human (H2H) interaction would become a powerful business model, as seen with LinkedIn? Staying abreast of these new dynamics is critical as the space continuously evolves.

There are situations when platforms often outpace traditional products by minimizing operational burdens. Consider platform giants like Uber, which owns no taxis; Facebook, which creates no content; Airbnb, which holds no real estate; and Alibaba, which carries no inventory. These models reduce logistical demands but introduce more complex service models and composable, interdependent structures. Both platform users and providers must monitor these overlaps and differentiations within their markets, continuously adapting to evolving business models to bridge gaps and remain competitive.

Learning from established business models and their trajectories offers valuable insights into effective patterns to follow, particularly with ecosystem involvement, which is the next critical point of clarity.

Platform Approach and Ecosystem

Deciding whether to adopt an open or closed platform approach is a fundamental choice that shapes your ecosystem's development and your platform's future. An open platform invites external developers, partners, and users to contribute and innovate, potentially accelerating growth and fostering a vibrant ecosystem. However, it also requires careful governance to maintain quality and security. On the other hand, a closed platform allows for more control and uniformity, enabling tighter integration and a more consistent user experience, but it might limit the pace of innovation and restrict the ecosystem's growth.

The choice between an open or closed platform approach should align with your broader business goals and the nature of your industry. For example, companies like Google have embraced an open approach with Android, creating a vast ecosystem of apps and services that have propelled the platform's growth. Conversely, Apple's iOS represents a more closed approach, prioritizing control and consistency, which has allowed for a highly curated ecosystem and a uniform user experience. However, in recent years, Apple has begun to open up its app store ecosystem by allowing creators to contribute and become profitable with the introduction of integrated tools and frameworks. This shift demonstrates Apple's recognition of the value in a more collaborative ecosystem, while still maintaining its strong emphasis on quality and security.

This decision also impacts how you engage with your ecosystem. An open approach may attract a broader range of partners and users, but it also demands robust mechanisms for managing contributions and ensuring compatibility. A closed approach, while limiting external contributions, can streamline operations and enhance security, making it easier to manage the platform as it scales.

Ultimately, the choice between open, closed, or middle ground should be guided by your platform's strategic goals, the competitive landscape, and the needs of your users. Whether you choose to open your doors wide or keep them tightly controlled, understanding the implications of this decision is crucial for long-term platform success.

Platform Technology Decisions

Technology decisions are at the heart of your platform strategy, playing a pivotal role in shaping its success. Often, organizations overlook or fail to be intentional about these decisions, leading to a spiral effect that hinders actual platform realization. Therefore, it's even more critical to approach these choices thoughtfully. These decisions involve selecting the right technologies, defining user experiences, and setting operational priorities. However, it's not just about making these choices once—continuous assessment and adaptation are crucial to stay aligned with your business goals, enhance efficiency, and drive sustainable growth.

A well-defined platform strategy should carefully consider the broad implications of technology decision-making and its impact. This process requires someone with deep technical expertise to formulate, drive, and create platform roadmaps that not only integrate with existing systems but also keep an eye on market dynamics and evolving technological perspectives.

Key components of this decision-making process include:

- **Technology Selection**: Choosing the right technologies that align with your business objectives and support the platform's long-term vision is essential. This includes not only selecting tools and frameworks but also considering scalability, interoperability with other platforms, and future-proofing. Keeping these choices grounded in your existing technology approach ensures practicality, avoiding the pitfalls of pursuing something impractical.

- **Security and Regulation**: These are non-negotiable elements of any platform strategy. Unfortunately, many organizations today still struggle with integrating security and regulatory compliance into their platforms, often treating them as afterthoughts. This is a critical mistake, especially as AI/ML technologies become more prevalent and bring their own set of challenges. Security and compliance should be built into the platform from the ground up, ensuring that they are accessible, understandable, and effective.

- **R&D and Experimentation**: For some organizations, having a dedicated core technology experimentation group or specialized R&D department is crucial. These teams provide early testing and adoption pathways for new technologies, ensuring that the platform stays ahead of the curve. It's vital to carefully consider how the learnings from experimentation are incorporated into the broader platform teams, as this can significantly impact the platform's innovation and adaptability.

- **Intellectual Property (IP) Strategy**: Your platform strategy should also include a strong focus on IP. Your products, trademarks, intellectual properties (IPs), and copyrights are vital assets that protect your innovations and distinguish your brand. By integrating IP considerations into your platform strategy, you safeguard your competitive edge while fostering an environment that encourages growth and innovation.

Once these foundational aspects are addressed, the next step is to integrate your network effects, partners, and other ecosystems into your technology strategy. At this stage of crafting a platform strategy, it's important to establish broad technology development, maintenance, and nurturing plans. Based on these, a separate detailed technology strategy should later be created (more on this in Chapter 9). Finally, it's essential to ensure that your platform teams are equipped and aligned to execute these strategies effectively.

Organizational Structure

Alfred Chandler, the renowned business historian, famously observed that "structure follows strategy." This principle is especially relevant in the context of successful platform patterns, where the platform strategy dictates organizational structure, governance, technology selection, and decision-making processes. A well-aligned organizational structure supports the long-term viability of your platform strategy and has a significant impact on your business model. By effectively managing strategy with structure and governance, you can ensure that the rest of the elements fall into place according to the Platform Success Blueprint.

The debate between centralized and decentralized models, as well as distributed versus shared governance, is crucial in understanding how to best allocate decision-making authority, maintain agility, and foster innovation. A centralized model may offer more control and consistency, while a decentralized model can encourage greater flexibility and responsiveness to market changes. The choice depends on the platform's goals, complexity, and the need for collaboration across teams and external partners.

Centralized vs. Decentralized Structure

- Centralized Structure: This model is characterized by a hierarchical setup where decisions are made by a central authority, often with a focus on keeping the business, products, or services centrally regulated. While this approach ensures uniformity and control, it may lack flexibility and constrain innovation.

- Decentralized Structure: In contrast, a decentralized structure empowers various departments or units to make decisions independently. This fosters innovation and enables rapid responses to changes. However, it can also lead to inconsistencies, tech silos, or isolated "technology islands" across the organization.

Distributed vs. Shared Governance

- Distributed Governance: This brings agility and localized

decision-making, allowing for quicker responses to specific needs, but it lacks centralized oversight, which can lead to inconsistencies and challenges in maintaining a unified strategy.

- Shared Governance: Involves collaborative decision-making processes where stakeholders at different levels and areas share responsibility and authority. This model promotes inclusivity and broad-based buy-in but can be slower in execution.

Let's explore the balancing act between structure and governance for platform teams.

Platform teams that have ownership of the platform tend to be more effective than segregated teams within a business. In my experience, involving core business functions and teams (as discussed in Chapter 6) in the right proportion and with the appropriate level of awareness is crucial for keeping your platform relevant and avoiding misconceptions.

A 2021 HBR article[8] found that platform companies significantly outperform traditional firms in profitability and efficiency, despite employing fewer workers. The study also highlighted a critical shortage of essential platform roles, as evidenced by the analysis of 11,080 platform job postings from 2,700 companies worldwide. This shortage underlines the growing demand for platform expertise, as companies strive to integrate increasingly complex technologies. Moreover, the study warned that companies focusing solely on internal operations may struggle to advance, further emphasizing the need for external engagement and collaboration.

Once platform teams and structures are in place, leaders should adopt a 'platform-thinking' approach to ensure success. This means ensuring that the Platform Success Blueprint is well understood and consistently communicated across all teams. Executives must also align long-term technology strategies with both internal capabilities and external market conditions to effectively integrate new technologies. Studies show that a lack of such alignment can lead to common issues. For example, research from HFS highlights that many cloud strategies fail due to misalignment with broader platform strategies, often resulting in siloed implementations that negatively impact numerous companies[9].

The best advice I can offer in this space is to let your structure follow your strategy, not the other way around. This means your organizational structure should be designed to support and enhance your strategic goals, rather than allowing existing structures to dictate your strategy. Second, the most successful models tend to favour decentralized teams with shared governance. This approach enables agility and responsiveness at the team level while maintaining alignment and cohesion across the organization through collaborative decision-making. Third, adopt platform thinking by communicating your platform strategy widely and consistently.

Defining the right structure to manage platform functions and governance is essential for nurturing growth. Technology is complex, but when you add humans to the equation, the complexity becomes immeasurable. I'll leave it to your best judgment which one challenges us more—and how to best balance both with the right mix of structure and governance.

Platform Metrics

Measurement and Metrics are vital for making informed, data-driven decisions in the technology space. They provide insights into performance, help identify potential issues, and optimize usage. For any platform to succeed, it's crucial to integrate metrics principles and guidance into the platform strategy. This integration ensures platforms meet user expectations while driving continuous improvement.

Given that platforms are composed of various tools and technologies, it's crucial to understand the layers of dependencies involved when defining metrics. For instance, if dependencies require measuring the cumulative effects of multiple layers or components within the platform, simply defining failure rates can be misleading in the short term and may fail entirely if the system collapses.

To illustrate this, I once faced a situation where a bank's customers demanded gold-level application availability that matched the performance of their on-premise data center. However, the platform integrators spent months debating and brainstorming how to achieve this availability level without fully understanding the underlying cloud architecture and service dependencies that affected overall uptime. The focus on matching data center availability metrics overlooked deeper issues related to cloud service layers, rendering these metrics shallow and ineffective. Such oversights can frequently occur when defining platform metrics, and the specifics can vary from case to case.

Therefore, it cannot be overstated how important it is to use a platform metrics model to define meaningful metrics for each stage of the platform lifecycle. Explaining this in full detail is beyond the scope of this chapter, but more information can be found in [Appendix E].

In this chapter, we delved into the critical components that form the foundation of a successful platform strategy. We explored the importance of aligning platform functions with your core business domain, emphasizing that clarity in defining what your platform should and should not do is crucial for its long-term viability. We examined various business models, highlighting how choosing the right one can drive both innovation and sustained growth. The chapter also discussed the significance of ecosystem involvement, where the choice between open and closed (or middle ground) platform approaches can shape the trajectory of your platform's development.

Moreover, we considered the technological aspects of platform strategy, underscoring the need for thoughtful decisions regarding technology selection, security, regulatory compliance, and intellectual property. We also touched on organizational structure, noting how it should align with your platform strategy to ensure that all elements work cohesively towards your strategic goals.

As you build and refine your platform strategy, remember that it is not a one-time effort but an ongoing process of iteration and improvement. Metrics play a vital role in this, providing the data-driven insights needed to make informed decisions at every stage of the platform lifecycle.

As we transition to the next chapter, it's important to recognize that even the most well-crafted platform strategy hinges on how your platform is experienced by its users. Platform experience and economization (the next topic of discussion) are critical because they serve as your platform's window to the world, showcasing your innovations through user interfaces and interactions. This is where your platform truly comes to life, and where your users engage with and derive value from what you have built. In the next chapter, we will explore why platform experience matters so much, and how it directly influences user satisfaction, retention, and ultimately, the success of your platform.

Key Takeaways

- The most critical measure of your platform's success starts with a simple question—do you have a clearly defined strategy? Without a clear strategy, your platform is likely to struggle right from the start.

- Even if you have a strategy, it's vital to ensure that it's genuinely relevant to your platform. A common mistake I've seen is the creation of loosely coupled frameworks that don't align with the platform mindset, or vice versa. Ensuring coherence between your strategy and engineering is crucial.

- The success of your platform strategy hinges on choosing the right business model, making informed technology decisions, nurturing the platform through its ecosystem, and crafting a compelling experience for all stakeholders.

- Essential elements of a strong platform strategy are outlined with an opinionated template to guide you, whether you're just beginning or looking to refine your approach.

- Ensure your platform metrics are both relevant and seamlessly integrated into your overall strategy.

---

1. https://www.hfsresearch.com/research/your-cloud-transformation-will-fail-if-it-is-not-grounded-in-business-objectives/

2. https://hbr.org/podcast/2011/01/ebays-ceo-on-growth-acquisitio

3. https://hbr.org/2009/12/lessons-from-myspace

4. https://www.applicoinc.com/blog/ge-digital-failed/

5. https://www.theguardian.com/technology/2015/nov/12/blackberry-ceo-john-chen-security-priv#:~:text=The%20CEO%20of%20troubled%20smartphone,from%20the%20edge%20of%20death%E2%80%9D

6. https://techcrunch.com/2021/10/19/automattic-tc1-acquisitions/

7. https://www.theverge.com/2020/6/22/21299032/microsoft-mixer-closing-facebook-gaming-partnership-xcloud-features

8. https://hbr.org/2019/05/a-study-of-more-than-250-platforms-reveals-why-most-fail

9. https://www.hfsresearch.com/research/your-cloud-transformation-will-fail-if-it-is-not-grounded-in-business-objectives/

Chapter Eight

Optimizing Platform Experience and Economization

"Master the art of user experience, and you'll hold all the cards."

Every platform, regardless of its type, delivers some form of user experience. This experience can manifest through interfaces, integrations, support, or operations. The way these experiences are delivered can make or break a platform's success. As platforms are designed to scale and offer repeatable, adaptable experiences, it's crucial to think beyond traditional customer-facing or UX/UI interactions. It's about optimizing every aspect of the experience, including how efficiently these interactions are delivered. This is the key point this chapter will explore in detail.

Platform experience is about seamlessly addressing user needs. When combined with resource optimization—ensuring efficiency at every level—you create platforms that become indispensable to users' lives. This principle applies not only to giants like Amazon, Netflix, and Apple but to any tech-driven platform. For example, Slack leverages cloud-native technologies to deliver seamless communication while optimizing resources through scalable, flexible services. Similarly, Zoom has optimized its platform for high-quality video conferencing with minimal latency, efficiently managing infrastructure through cloud services to support millions of users.

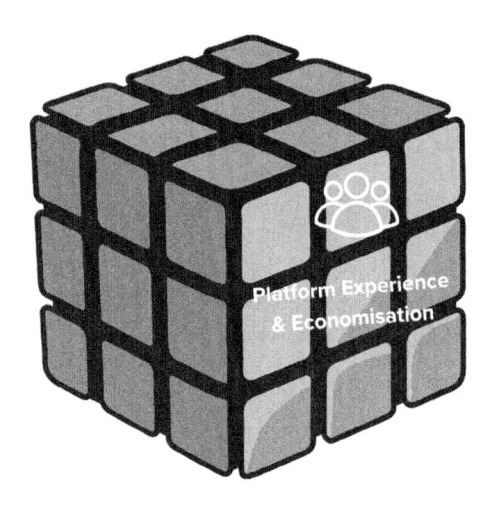

Economizing the User Experience

Economizing the user experience reflects the strength of your core business and platform strategy. Efficiently managing user experience can be the difference between a sustainable, scalable platform and one that struggles to keep up with its operational demands. It's not just about what you offer—whether a product, service, or documentation—but how efficiently you deliver it. By economizing resources like money, time, and effort, companies can streamline processes, reduce costs, and enhance operational efficiency. Automation tools minimize manual intervention, while scalable cloud services reduce infrastructure demands. Without effective economizing, even the best user experience won't guarantee long-term success. Strategic economizing keeps your platform cost-effective while maintaining high-quality service delivery.

This aspect of the blueprint encapsulates your brand's identity and how it interfaces with users, applying equally to both customer-facing platforms and internal systems. For instance, a business platform, such as e-commerce, might showcase product listings and return policies, while **Internal Developer Platforms (IDPs)** integrate developer workflows and influence the growth and pace of the business. These internal platforms are essential to ensuring that developers can work efficiently, which ultimately impacts the user-facing experience.

The Importance of Platform Experience

The outward-facing element of the platform experience forms the first impression and the ongoing interaction point with customers, driving engagement and satisfaction. However, companies that excel in marketing and strategy but neglect their platform experience—particularly internal platforms—may struggle with platform adoption and overall success.

This side of the blueprint covers user experience (UX), user interface (UI), financial models, financial operations (FinOps), technical operations (TechOps), customer operations, platform SLAs, and user satisfaction. While UX/UI ensures the platform is intuitive and engaging, operational aspects like FinOps and TechOps manage efficiency and growth. Customer operations focus on delivering excellent support and maintaining SLAs to ensure long-term user satisfaction and loyalty.

Let's explore these aspects of platform experience and economizing further.

Platform Experience: The Core of User Engagement

Platform experience is crucial for both internal and external users, encompassing everything from user interactions to platform operations and support channels. A seamless and intuitive experience is vital, whether it's customers interacting with the platform or developers building it.

To understand the importance of a cohesive platform experience, consider the difference between **Digital Experience Platforms (DXPs)** and traditional **Content Management Systems (CMSs)**. DXPs go beyond just managing content—they unify data and content to create personalized customer journeys across multiple channels. For instance, platforms like Amazon or Netflix offer seamless journeys across devices, maintaining data integrity and providing continuity, whether users are completing a transaction or resuming a movie.

Many firms are rethinking their roles, envisioning themselves not just as providers of products and services, but as enablers of platforms that allow customers to create their own experiences and value. This shift helps companies meet the ideal of delivering what customers want, when and how they want it[1]. Successful companies like Pinterest and Salesforce exemplify this model by allowing users to craft their own experiences within clearly defined and governed interfaces.

A strong brand sets clear customer expectations and delivers on its promises. Consider BMW's "The Ultimate Driving Machine" or Lego's "Endless Play." These slogans encapsulate the brand's essence and promise. Unfortunately, this branding aspect is often overlooked in platform development. Organizations should integrate their brand's identity into the platform's design and experience. If a platform promises simplicity, every aspect of its interface and user experience should reflect that simplicity.

The platform experience must cater to all user types—be it consumers, users, or internal developers. Each role is vital, contributing to the network effects that help platforms scale. A developer ecosystem that finds a platform easy to work with will create more tools and integrations, enhancing the experience for end users and creating a virtuous cycle of growth and engagement.

UX/UI design should reflect the business purpose, brand identity, and user roles. Since your customers interact through this layer, the platform must be user-friendly and aligned with your brand. Effective UX/UI design boosts usability and satisfaction, such as with e-commerce platforms that offer easy navigation, quick checkout, and personalized recommendations. Companies like Shopify, WordPress, and Squarespace provide customizable UX/UI templates that businesses can adapt to match their brand and functional requirements.

By focusing on seamless user experience, unified content management, strong brand integration, and catering to all user types, organizations can create platforms that exceed user expectations, driving satisfaction and loyalty.

Platform Operations and Support: Extending the Experience

Customer operations and support can vary in scope depending on the complexity of your offerings. Effective support includes multiple touchpoints like live chat, email, phone support, and social media interactions. Platforms like Adobe Experience Cloud, Zendesk, Freshdesk, and Intercom offer integrated solutions to manage customer inquiries, track support tickets, and provide comprehensive analytics, ensuring timely and effective resolution of customer issues, which enhances satisfaction and loyalty.

Typically, Level 1 and Level 2 support are handled through this pillar of the platform strategy. More complex technical issues are escalated to the platform engineering teams, ensuring that deeper problems are debugged and resolved by experts. For instance, if you use a website development platform from a third party, the initial support stages are handled by the business, while technical issues or advanced integrations are managed by the platform engineers/teams.

Economization: Optimizing Resources for Efficiency

Economizing—what does it mean? At its core, it's about optimizing every aspect of your platform to save on costs, time, effort, and resources, without compromising quality, performance, or user experience. This involves making strategic decisions that streamline operations, reduce waste, and enhance productivity, ensuring resources are used as efficiently and sustainably as possible.

Automation plays a crucial role in economizing, driving scalability, efficiency, and innovation. By integrating automation with cost awareness into your economizing plan, you create a system that not only operates efficiently today but is also prepared to scale and adapt to future demands.

Let's explore the three key aspects of economizing: time, cost, and effort.

Economization of Time

The pace at which you innovate and scale is directly tied to the time invested in your platform. Time is a crucial resource that often determines the success or failure of a platform. Efficient time management varies depending on whether you are a platform user or a platform provider. For platform users, time translates to experience and engagement. The more streamlined and intuitive a platform is, the less time users spend struggling with it, allowing them to focus on maximizing their experience.

For platform providers, economizing time involves investing in automation and creating easily integrable interfaces that reduce friction in the development process. Automating repetitive tasks, streamlining workflows, and minimizing deployment cycles are essential strategies. Tools like Jenkins or GitHub Actions, for example, can automate the build, test, and deployment phases, significantly reducing the manual effort required. This not only speeds up the development process but also ensures consistency and reliability in the platform's output.

To fully capitalize on this potential, organizations must develop a robust platform strategy that prioritizes the pace and depth of time investment. This includes both technical implementation and human aspects—investing in skilled professionals who can effectively manage and optimize time-saving technologies.

Economization of Cost

The cost of platforms is often overlooked in the early stages due to their complexity and variability. Typically, challenges such as assembling teams and navigating the nuances of the technology take priority, leaving platform cost considerations on the back burner. Platforms are inherently a composition of features, tools, technologies, and the experiences they aim to create, leading to a wide range of potential costs.

For platform users, the total cost of ownership (TCO) can be elusive, particularly when considering the platform's features. Users may overlook the additional expenses required for necessary integrations, time, and effort, leading to unanticipated costs. For instance, using a third-party platform might seem cost-effective at first, but hidden costs related to scaling, feature add-ons, or specialized integrations can dramatically increase the TCO over time.

Similarly, for platform providers, economizing costs revolves around strategically reducing expenses while maximizing value. Cloud providers like AWS (Amazon Web Services) or Microsoft Azure offer pay-as-you-go models and a broad range of services, which can help reduce upfront infrastructure costs. However, the TCO is often underestimated due to the additional expenses associated with utilizing these services.

To effectively economize costs, businesses need to implement robust cost management practices. This includes continuous monitoring of cloud usage, setting up automated alerts for cost thresholds, and leveraging governance.

Formula for Success with Cost Management

There is no one-size-fits-all formula for managing costs in complex and large multi-platform scenarios. However, successful patterns do exist, and platform companies can develop effective strategies for achieving cost efficiency and sustainability. Here are some key approaches:

- **Focused Ninjas**: Expecting everyone in the organization to naturally assume cost responsibility and frugality is a common mistake. Instead, platform companies should establish a core group—referred to as "Focused Ninjas"—who specialize in cost management. These individuals quickly develop the skills to optimize costs and are responsible for educating the rest of the organization on cost-saving measures. The focus should extend beyond cost planning and visibility to fostering a cost-conscious culture throughout the company.

- **Implement Predictive Analytics:** Leverage data-driven insights to forecast demand, optimize resource allocation, and anticipate potential cost overruns. Predictive analytics can identify underutilized resources or areas where costs are likely to spike, enabling timely adjustments to keep spending in check. By automating the detection of high-cost mistakes or potential errors through predictive analysis, you can proactively prevent issues and maintain efficiency. This is a highly effective approach that benefits everyone involved.

- **Automate Cost Management**: Adopt a consumption-driven approach from the outset by incorporating automation to manage costs effectively. Automate tasks such as resource scaling, budget tracking, and alerting for cost anomalies, reducing the burden on human resources while ensuring accurate and timely cost control, whether for platform users or internal cost attribution.

- **Invest in Security and Compliance**: While it may seem like an added expense, investing in robust security protocols and ensuring compliance with industry standards can prevent costly breaches and fines. Regularly updating these measures will protect your platform and save money in the long run by avoiding the financial repercussions of security incidents.

- **Prioritize High-ROI R&D Projects**: Focus on research and development projects that offer the highest potential return on investment (ROI) and significant market impact. By channelling resources into these high-value projects, platform companies can maximize their financial returns while minimizing waste on less impactful initiatives.

- **Make Compatible Choices:** Choose tools and vendors that seamlessly integrate with your existing ecosystem and provide transparent cost visibility (more on this in the next chapter on Technology Strategy and Ecosystem). Ensuring compatibility can streamline operations and improve cost management.

Economization of Efforts

Effort economizing focuses on maximizing productivity by automating platform management tasks. Technologies like Kubernetes reduce manual intervention in areas such as scaling and load balancing. However, the complexity of Kubernetes can limit these benefits if not managed by skilled professionals. This topic will be explored in depth in Chapter 11.

So far, we have explored platform experience and economization. Now, let's look at some opportunities to learn from a few real-world examples:

Enhancing User Experience: Key Opportunities

- **Opportunity 1 - Enhancing Cost Visibility and Control**: Implementing advanced cost tracking and management tools helps maintain financial discipline and optimize spending. *Example*: Netflix's efficient cost management strategies allowed it to streamline operations and outperform competitors like Blockbuster, which struggled with higher operational costs.

- **Opportunity 2 - Embracing New Experiences and Technologies**: Adopting innovative technologies and practices enables continuous improvement and cost efficiency. *Example*: Companies that embraced digital photography, such as Canon and Sony, successfully transitioned and thrived, in contrast to Kodak's challenges. Nokia's resurgence with new technology adoption showcases how embracing change can lead to renewed market relevance.

- **Opportunity 3 - Strategic Scaling for Growth**: Effective planning and execution in scaling infrastructure ensures smooth performance and user satisfaction. *Example*: Facebook's robust scaling strategies allowed it to accommodate rapid growth, positioning it ahead of competitors like MySpace, which faced challenges in scaling effectively.

- **Opportunity 4 - Economizing Through Robust Security Investments: Investing in strong security measures is not just a safeguard but a strategic way to economize. By proactively protecting against breaches, companies can avoid the substantial costs associated with data loss, fines, and damage control. This approach ensures that resources are allocated efficiently, thereby reducing the long-term financial impact of potential security incidents. Example: Companies like Google and Microsoft, which prioritize cybersecurity (despite occasional challenges), have not only protected their reputation and finances but also economized by preventing the expensive repercussions that befell companies like Equifax[2] (which suffered a massive breach in 2017 due to inadequate security measures, resulting in severe financial and reputational damage).

- **Opportunity 5 - Optimizing Customer Support Management**: Efficient customer support processes reduce costs and enhance satisfaction. Example: Companies like Amazon and Zappos (a subsidiary of Amazon, known for its outstanding customer service) are renowned for their exceptional customer service, which not only reduces operational costs but also drives customer loyalty and market leadership.

Experience and Economizing: The Platform Reflection

Your platform reflects your business strategy, influencing both your ecosystem and company culture. Clear documentation, seamless user interfaces, and efficient operations enhance user satisfaction while optimizing resources.

By focusing on experience and economizing time, money, and effort, you can create and maintain platforms that are not only efficient and scalable but also cost-effective, driving business success.

Key Takeaways

- Deliberately design and detail the user experience to ensure it aligns with your platform's goals and user expectations. Provide a seamless experience for both external and internal users.

- Wherever possible, allow users to personalize their experience, fostering creativity and engagement.

- Develop your platform with scalability in mind, while economizing time, resources, and effort from the outset to ensure long-term efficiency and sustainability.

- Never economize on something that fails you; user experience and operations reflect your stability with platform technology. This includes the financial model and operational model. Sharpen your saw.

1. https://hbr.org/2012/05/turn-your-company-into-a-custo
2. https://www.ftc.gov/enforcement/refunds/equifax-data-breach-settlement

Section C

Platform Success Patterns - For Providers

Chapter Nine

Mastering Technology Strategy and Ecosystem

"When a business dreams big, technology builds the ladder. The trick is balancing the climb!"

Technology strategy is about selecting and nurturing the right set of technical tools and solutions to build and integrate platforms. While this may be selectively applicable to platform users, it is essential for platform providers. A robust technology strategy requires a well-defined platform strategy as its foundation. This strategy influences your approach to technology selection, skill set requirements, involvement, and long-term decision-making. It also shapes your innovation trajectory, directs your focus, and drives your growth within the ecosystem. Your technology strategy should align with existing capabilities while remaining adaptable, reflecting your growth through platform technology and ecosystem relationships.

Technology Strategy vs. Platform Strategy

Before we proceed, let's clarify a common question: How do platform strategy and technology strategy differ—aren't they the same? The short answer is no, they are distinct, and every platform company must maintain them separately to ensure long-term growth and business agility.

Platform strategy, covered in detail in Chapter 7, focuses on the platform's business model and core capabilities. It addresses key questions such as whether you need a platform, whether it should be internal or external, and whether to keep it open or closed. These are foundational decisions that shape the direction and scope of your platform.

In contrast, technology strategy zooms in on selecting the tools and technologies that will support and execute the platform strategy. This is where you decide, among numerous technology options, which combination will best align with and enable your platform strategy. This chapter delves into the process of creating a technology strategy and leveraging the power of your ecosystem to support it.

Introduction to Platform Technology Strategy

Technology decisions today are no longer about making a single set of choices; they involve navigating the increasing granularity that has emerged as a byproduct of innovation and globalization. This complexity requires organizations to carefully balance the selection of both new and existing technologies. It has also deepened partnerships between technology organizations, moving beyond mere service or product support to more integrated collaborations. At the same time, leveraging the open ecosystem—now a greater source of technology innovation than any single vendor—has become a critical dynamic to consider.

This chapter will explore these important aspects and examine what platform users and providers need to be aware of in order to fully integrate an open ecosystem, partners, and nurture their technology stack effectively. It's important to clarify that this chapter won't prescribe specific tools, vendors, or platforms, but it will guide you in making informed platform technology decisions at the right level of detail. For instance, if your strategy involves launching a global e-commerce platform, building a custom payment gateway would be unnecessary when established solutions like Stripe or PayPal can be seamlessly integrated and tailored to your needs. Similarly, if your platform strategy includes implementing AI-driven analytics, it would be more efficient to leverage existing AI frameworks or partner with established providers like Google Cloud AI or Microsoft Azure AI, rather than building an AI platform from scratch—unless you have the strategy, expertise, and time to support such an endeavor.

Understanding the technology implications is crucial before making or continuing your selection. A well-defined technology strategy keeps you focused on the essential learning, practice, and nurturing required for success.

Technology Decision Framework

The key elements of a technology strategy for platforms comprise seven core principles:

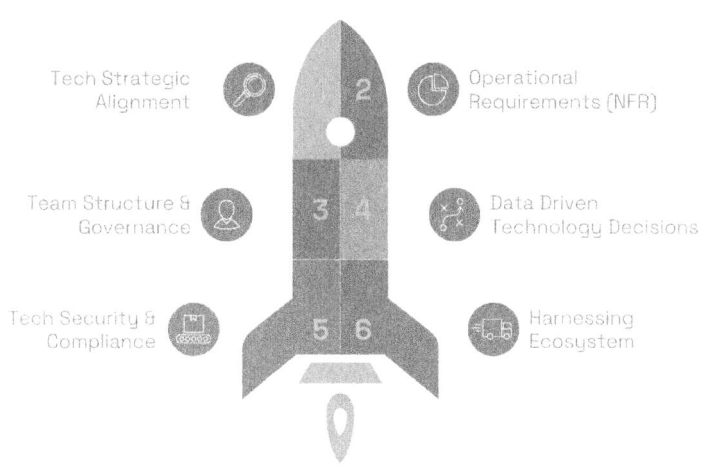

Technology Decision Framework

Strategic Alignment

While this point has been discussed earlier, it's crucial to reinforce that technology choices should be driven by how well they align with platform objectives and, in turn, with the company's long-term business goals. Teams must assess whether a technology supports their strategic initiatives, such as digital transformation, customer engagement, scale or market expansion. You might have three different tools that your developers are eager to use, but do you want to manage the lifecycle integration of all three simultaneously? The decision depends on the value these tools add, the costs they incur, and the effort they require.

I've seen platform teams struggle not due to a lack of learning or skills, but because of poor technology choices that later require substantial effort to bridge gaps. This can happen for various reasons: Sometimes, there isn't someone with enough experience to make the right decisions and communicate the vision across teams. Other times, projects begin in startup mode, forcing continuous evolution to keep up, or organizational complexity adds to the challenges. Some companies falter when overwhelmed by too many options, while others thrive by streamlining their development with a select few tools. In large organizations, strong opinions often lead to different choices, creating tech islands—or organizational silos—and other complications. Almost invariably, I've seen large companies grapple with these issues, often struggling to strike a balance between new and old technologies while aligning their technology choices with their overall strategy.

Operational Requirements (or Non-Functional Requirements)

Selecting technology based solely on functional suitability often leaves gaps that can become operationally challenging for platform development and operations. Addressing operational requirements during the selection process helps manage the unknowns and unseen implications of the technology, requiring careful consideration. Key non-functional aspects to consider in technology selection include the following, though they may vary depending on the specific case and could involve other non-functional aspects ('ilities') as well:

1. **Scalability**: Companies need to evaluate whether the technology can scale with the growth of the business. This includes its ability to handle increased loads, users, and data volumes.

2. **Integration**: The ease of integrating new technology

with existing systems and processes is crucial. Companies should prefer technology solutions that offer robust APIs or other interoperability methods with their current tech stack.

3. **Reliability and Performance**: Performance metrics, uptime guarantees, and overall reliability are key factors. Technologies that demonstrate high performance and minimal downtime are preferred.

4. **Financial Considerations:**

    - Total Cost of Ownership (TCO): Companies must calculate the total cost of ownership, which includes not just the purchase price but also implementation, maintenance, training, and operational costs.

    - Return on Investment (ROI): Projected ROI is a significant factor. Technologies that promise a high return on investment by improving efficiency, reducing costs, or driving revenue growth are preferred.

Technology Teams – Structure and Governance

Different technology teams align with various team structures and governance models based on multiple factors. These broad definitions are usually established at the platform strategy level, as we have sufficiently discussed in Chapter 7. However, at this stage, the technology strategy should guide the alignment of team responsibilities to ensure they support the platform's strategic goals. The strategy should enforce good practices and governance, ensuring that platform teams operate like coordinated players on an assembly line, rather than overlapping in concerns and responsibilities.

The technology strategy builds on the platform strategy to further define team structures, communication channels, and guardrails, ensuring that each team understands its role in the broader ecosystem. The core idea behind platforms and platform teams is to automate and encapsulate tasks to a level that allows flexibility between groups, even if not in perfect detail.

That being said, it's important to recognize that, when it comes to complexity, human factors often outweigh technological ones. Therefore, platform teams must leverage strategic clarity and reinforcement to navigate these challenges effectively.

Earlier in this book (Chapter 2), we explored six decades of innovation patterns in the platform space. One challenge that has remained constant throughout these decades is the critical importance of security and compliance. As cyber threats continue to escalate, these concerns have only grown more pressing. Therefore, when evaluating technology solutions, security features must be a top priority. Companies need to thoroughly assess whether the technology can protect sensitive data and comply with necessary security standards.

When selecting a technology or vendor, it's essential to evaluate how securely data moves in and out of the system, whether data encryption is in place, and whether appropriate access levels are maintained to meet your platform standards. For instance, Apple devices are built with security as a core principle, ensuring that not only are their own devices secure by design, but they also avoid introducing security vulnerabilities when integrating with other technology solutions by ensuring proper abstraction at the integration layer.

Regulatory compliance is another non-negotiable aspect. Adhering to industry regulations and standards such as GDPR, HIPAA, or PCI is mandatory. While these requirements may seem rigid and challenging to navigate, they can be effectively addressed by incorporating them early in your technology decisions and design approach. Technologies that facilitate or ensure compliance with these regulations should be preferred. In nearly all of my experiences, treating these requirements as an afterthought has led to production delays, regulatory setbacks, and the need to revisit the drawing board, ultimately accumulating technical debt and requiring patches or delays at later stages.

To manage these aspects effectively, it's crucial to involve experts who have a deep understanding of both technology design and regulatory requirements at the right stages—early on, throughout the development process, and on an ongoing basis. Balancing these factors is key to ensuring that your platform remains secure and compliant even in an increasingly complex digital landscape.

Data-Driven Technology Decisions

When strengthening technology frameworks, it's essential to prioritize user experience and continuous feedback. Technologies that are user-friendly and require minimal training are more likely to be adopted successfully, leading to higher satisfaction rates. By actively incorporating feedback from employees and stakeholders—those directly impacted by the technology—companies can ensure better adoption and utilization. Additionally, selecting technologies with strong innovation potential and a clear roadmap for future development is crucial for staying ahead in a rapidly evolving market. Future-proofing these technologies—ensuring they can adapt to emerging trends and changes—helps avoid frequent upgrades and replacements, ultimately enhancing long-term strategic agility.

How you expose and manage your data through technology layers significantly influences how effectively you leverage that data to drive decisions. This aspect has become even more critical with advancements in Generative AI (GenAI) and machine learning integration within the platform industry—a topic we will explore further in Chapter 15.

Moreover, all technology decisions should be grounded in data and measured facts, whether evaluating the effectiveness of a POC (Proof of Concept) or MVP (Minimum Viable Product) or conducting a comprehensive technology effectiveness check. Through data-driven decision-making and continuous adaptation based on user input, organizations can create robust and forward-looking technology environments.

Consider this example from a platform project I worked on for a major U.S. telecom company. We ran into a major issue with vendor technology compatibility. The telecom giant had finalized certain technologies for their platform, only to discover later that the vendors they were integrating with couldn't provide the necessary support for integration. This created a "black hole" scenario, leading to substantial delays and requiring significant effort to build patches and close the gaps. On top of that, we had to guide the vendor through modernization efforts, which was well beyond the original project scope.

This experience highlights the critical importance of conducting thorough compatibility checks early on—during the MVP or technology selection phases—to avoid costly delays and complications later.

This seemingly simple yet crucial step is often overlooked by platform teams. Defining these principles within your technology strategy and ensuring they're communicated and implemented across all teams during integration is key to preventing such issues.

Now, ask yourself: Does your organization have a well-documented and justified record of technology decisions? If not, this is the time to make it a priority—regardless of which stage or maturity of implementation you are in.

Harnessing Technology Ecosystems

Importance of Partner and Vendor Ecosystems

In today's technological landscape, choosing the right technology partner or vendor is crucial to the success of your platform. A strong vendor ecosystem provides more than just tools—it offers reliability, support, and a network of resources that ensure the technology can scale and adapt as needed. Vendor reputation and ecosystem strength are critical factors in technology selection, as organizations seek technologies from reputable vendors with proven track records of stability, support, and continuous improvement.

For instance, platforms like AWS, Azure, and Google Cloud have built robust ecosystems that allow businesses to leverage pre-built integrations and industry partnerships. These partnerships extend the capabilities of platforms, reduce development overhead, and allow businesses to innovate faster by focusing on value-added services rather than reinventing the wheel.

Collaborating within a well-established vendor ecosystem also defines your network effects—encompassing partnerships, community relationships, and influence within the ecosystem. These relationships are crucial for learning, support, and staying ahead in terms of technological innovations. For platform users, it's essential to carefully evaluate vendor ecosystems for their ability to meet both current and future needs, ensuring they align with your long-term platform strategy.

Importance of the Open Ecosystem

"Community is the lifeblood of open source, and open source is the engine of software innovation[1]," said Priyanka Sharma, Executive Director, CNCF.

The open ecosystem, particularly open-source communities, plays a foundational role in the development of modern platforms. Open-source technologies form the backbone of many businesses today, driving innovation through collaborative development. Organizations like the Linux Foundation, Cloud Native Computing Foundation (CNCF), and Apache Software Foundation are instrumental in creating core technologies, such as Linux, Kubernetes, and Apache Kafka, which have become integral components of commercial platforms like AWS, Azure, and Google Cloud.

The open ecosystem provides significant value by allowing companies to build on proven, widely-used technologies while contributing back to the community. This mutual collaboration fosters innovation, creates a robust support network, and accelerates technological advancements. However, businesses must stay vigilant, as changes in foundational open-source technologies can impact their platforms, requiring regular updates and adjustments.

Understanding and leveraging the open ecosystem is essential for platform success. Organizations should actively engage with open-source communities and contribute to their development, rather than passively relying on providers or integrators to make decisions for them. This engagement helps companies stay informed of the latest developments and trends, ensuring that their platforms remain up-to-date and competitive. Tools like the Gartner Hype Cycle and McKinsey Technology Trends report can help platform users navigate the complexities of the technology landscape, guiding them toward informed, strategic decisions that optimize platform usage.

To summarize, by integrating the following seven elements into your platform technology strategy—Strategic Alignment, Operational Requirements (NFRs), Structure & Governance, Data-Driven Decisions, Security & Compliance, and Leveraging Ecosystems—you can better navigate technology selection, adoption, and nurturing.

Every technology decision, whether intentional or not, shapes the non-functional aspects of your platform. For instance, challenges in scaling or expansion often stem from how your platform strategy influences technology choices, partnerships, and operations.

These decisions ultimately manifest in your applications and services, affecting their ability to scale and support growth, which in turn impacts the platform's reputation and success. Hence being intentional and taking control of your technology strategy is crucial to ensuring long-term success.

How to Use These Principles

The next big question is: how do you gauge technology, its impact, partnerships, and scalability? Can these factors be measured or assessed? The answer lies in developing a mechanism that you can continuously leverage. Here are three steps you can take immediately, no matter where you are in your platform journey.

Examine Your Tech Stack

Start by examining your current technology stack, or if you're beginning from scratch, finalize one. A typical technology stack for modern enterprises might look something like this, though its complexity can vary depending on organizational alignment and platform strategies—you get the idea:

Sample tech stack (only for reference)	
Languages	Java, C++, Go, JavaScript, Python, Dart, Kotlin
Frameworks	Angular, Spark, Quarkus
Middleware	Apache Kafka, Flutter
DBS	PostgreSQL, DynamoDB, MongoDB, AWS RedShift, AWS EMR, ElasticSearch
Public Cloud Services	AWS, Azure, Google
Tools	GitHub, Terraform, Artifactory, Jenkins, Sonar, JIRA, Confluence
Observability/ Monitoring	OpenTelemetry, Splunk, DataDog, Prometheus, Grafana, AppDynamics, Dynatrace
Security	SE Linux, eBPF, OPA, Cloud services
Data Analytics	Tableau, QlikView, Snowflake, Databricks
Machine Learning Services	GenAI services, Open Models, ML services

I strongly recommend maintaining clear visibility of your tech stack at all times. Whether it's a single page or multiple pages, a single table or divided by groups, it's crucial that this information is accessible across the entire engineering organization—developers, designers, architects, managers, and leaders alike. This document not only clarifies the choices made but also highlights any duplication and ensures the purpose and reasoning behind your tech stack are transparent at all levels. Surprisingly, in my experience, this seemingly straightforward information is often missing in organizations, regardless of their size or level.

Follow an Iterative Decision-Making Process

- **Assessment**: Identify and document the business needs and technical requirements.

- **Research and Evaluation**: Research available technologies, conduct pilot tests, and evaluate them based on defined criteria.

- **Stakeholder Involvement**: Engage the right stakeholders from various departments to gather input and ensure the selected technology meets cross-functional needs.

- **Cost-Benefit Analysis**: Perform a detailed cost-benefit analysis to compare the long-term value of different technologies.

- **Documenting Decision and Implementation**: Make a final decision and plan the implementation process, including timelines, training, and support.

- **Re-assessment**: Re-assess with a decided frequency (using a checkpoint format, such as the example given below).

Technology Decision Framework - Checklist

Use this template and tailor it to fit your technology strategy needs and business requirements.

1. **Strategic Alignment**

- Does this technology align with our long-term business goals and strategic initiatives?
- Does it support our vision for digital transformation and market expansion?
- **Decision Basis:** Go / No-Go

2. **Competitive Advantage**

- Can this technology provide a competitive edge, helping us innovate and differentiate in the market?
- **Decision Basis:** Go / No-Go

3. **Scalability**

- Is the technology scalable to handle expected growth in users, transactions, and data volume?
- Can it manage increased loads effectively?
- **Decision Basis:** Go / No-Go

4. **Integration**

- How easily does it integrate with existing systems and processes?
- Does it offer robust APIs and interoperability with our current tech stack?
- **Decision Basis:** Go / No-Go

5. **Total Cost of Ownership (TCO)**

    ○ What are the costs of implementation, maintenance, training, and operations?

    ○ Is the return on investment (ROI) justifiable?

    ○ **Decision Basis:** Go / No-Go

6. **Vendor Continuous Assessment**

    ○ How reliable and supportive is the vendor?

    ○ What is their track record in continuous improvement and customer service?

    ○ **Decision Basis:** Go / No-Go

7. **Security and Compliance**

    ○ Does the technology ensure data security and comply with industry regulations (e.g., GDPR, HIPAA)?

    ○ **Decision Basis:** Go / No-Go

8. **User Experience and Adoption**

    ○ Is the technology user-friendly, or does it require extensive training?

    ○ What feedback have we received from stakeholders about its usability?

    ○ **Decision Basis:** Go / No-Go

9. **Innovation and Future-Proofing**

    - Does the technology allow for future innovations and adaptability to market trends?

    - Is it likely to remain relevant in the long term?

    - **Decision Basis:** Go / No-Go

10. **Community and Ecosystem**

- How strong is the community and ecosystem around this technology?

- Can we leverage external support and innovations to add value?

- **Decision Basis:** Go / No-Go

Key Takeaways

- Use a technology decision framework to guide your technology strategy.

- Don't buy into technology promises—only invest if it aligns with your platform strategy and integrates smoothly with your existing tech stack.

- Leverage the ecosystem and contribute as a responsible participant.

- Have your technology department not just set the standards but also know the technology platforms and educate until the last person is educated in the value chain.

- Do not compromise on powerful operational and non-functional requirements if you want to scale bigger and bigger.

- Know your correct metrics and measure them as an audit or review every single quarter if not monthly.

---

1. https://www.forbes.com/sites/adrianbridgwater/2022/10/26/cncf-director-sharma-community-is-the-lifeblood-of-open-source/

Chapter Ten

Designing Effective Platform Architecture

"Building a platform takes effort, right? That's why it's worth investing the time to design it right!"

Design and architecture are the backbone of any platform. It's akin to architecting a building; while we can function in a poorly designed structure, the consequences are inevitable and often costly. Yet, despite knowing this, we frequently overlook the importance of proper architecture and the right foundation. Let's be honest: building a platform requires significant effort, so why not invest the necessary time and resources into sound design and architectural practices? This proactive approach saves us from the later hassle of patching, polishing, or fixing broken technology solutions.

From this point forward, the groundwork of platform realization begins, bringing challenges that are not only inevitable but also crucial to address head-on. As you progress through your platform experience (which we explored in Chapter 8), the significance of design and architecture will become increasingly apparent. The effectiveness of your platform implementation (which we'll delve into in Chapter 11) will put these principles to the test. This entire process is driven by your platform strategy and enriched by a deep understanding of platform technology, ensuring that you're not just building a platform, but building it right.

Platform architecture and design are about creating a solid, scalable foundation that aligns with your platform strategy and informs your technology strategy. It's about seamlessly integrating technologies, ensuring security and performance, and fostering innovation. This is where you should embed cost considerations and regulatory compliance as foundational elements, not as afterthoughts. It's not just about building for today but also about anticipating future needs, enabling growth, and delivering exceptional user experiences.

Platform providers create platforms for three broad purposes, each tailored to specific needs based on user types, exposure, and the desired balance between generative (creating new capabilities) and repetitive (standardizing and scaling existing capabilities) functions:

1. **Business Platform:** This type of platform integrates and delivers business applications, core domains, and features directly to consumers and users. For example, Uber's Rider App functions as a Business Platform, offering ride-hailing services by integrating core features such as booking, payment processing, and ride tracking.

2. **External Enablement Platform:** These platforms are designed to expose and orchestrate platform features, making them accessible to external users and systems. They enhance the network effects of a platform by attracting more users and partners. Examples from Uber include the Uber API, which allows external developers to integrate Uber's ride-hailing services into their apps, and the Marketplace Platform, which optimizes supply-demand matching, pricing algorithms, and driver routing to ensure efficient operations.

3. **Internal Enablement Platform:** This type of platform is designed to boost the agility and speed of both external and business platforms by empowering developers and

platform creators to work more efficiently. A notable example can be Uber's Observability and Monitoring Platform, which offers engineers real-time system insights, ensuring high performance and reliability across Uber's services (with more details covered in the next chapter).

Each of these platform types serves a distinct purpose, enhancing the overall effectiveness and scalability of the platform ecosystem. Additionally, each platform caters to different types of consumers or users—whether technical or non-technical—based on how they interact with the platform. As a result, platform architecture and design approaches vary accordingly.

Before diving into the different architectural essentials, let's explore some must-know platform design principles. These principles can then be combined with the design approach, required design elements, and design patterns. All of these will be gradually unfolded in the next few sections. Let's dive in.

Platform Design Principles

While architectural patterns and design elements may vary between platforms, certain design principles remain universally important. These serve as essential guidelines for platform architects and engineers. Depending on your platform's needs and context, you can build on or adapt these principles.

Modularity and Decoupling

This principle emphasizes designing platforms with modular components that operate independently. Each module can be developed, tested, and scaled separately, enhancing flexibility and enabling continuous platform evolution. Microservices architecture is a prime example, where the platform is broken down into smaller, independently deployable services, simplifying maintenance and reducing the risk of system-wide failures.

Module A	Module B	Module C
User Interface	Business Logic	Data Access

Scalability and Elasticity

Platforms should be designed to handle increasing demands by scaling both vertically and horizontally. This is crucial for accommodating growth in user numbers, data volumes, and transaction loads without compromising performance. Technologies like AWS Fargate and event-driven architectures allow platforms to dynamically scale resources based on real-time demand, ensuring efficient use of resources while maintaining a seamless user experience.

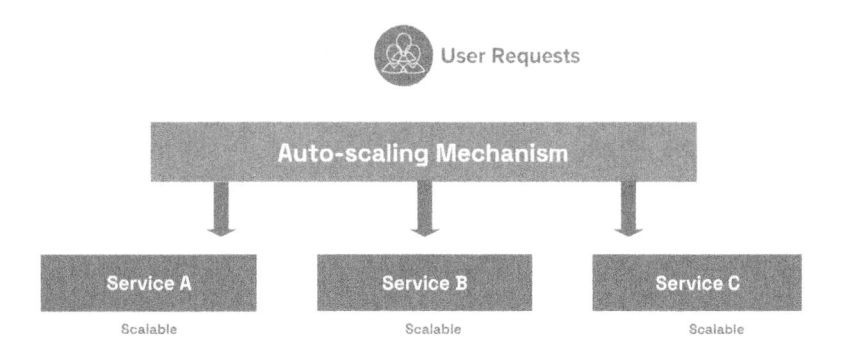

Resilience and Fault Tolerance

Resilience and fault tolerance are built into platforms to ensure continuous operation, even when components fail. Platforms designed for fault tolerance can withstand failures without affecting overall service availability. Netflix's microservices architecture, combined with its "Chaos Engineering" practices, exemplifies this principle by regularly testing and improving resilience across its platform.

Security by Design

Security should be integrated into every layer of the platform architecture from the outset. This proactive approach protects against vulnerabilities, ensures compliance with regulations, and maintains user trust. Apple's iOS exemplifies this principle by enforcing strict controls over app development and integration to safeguard user data and privacy.

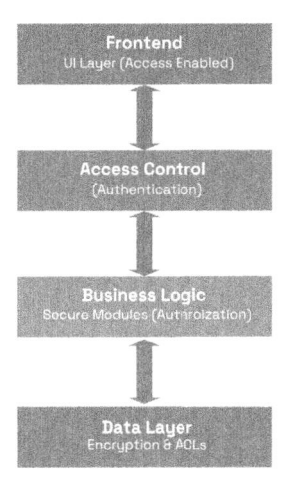

Interoperability and Integration

This principle ensures that platforms can seamlessly integrate with other systems, platforms, and services. Using standardized APIs and protocols facilitates integration, allowing the platform to expand its ecosystem and collaborate with third parties. Kubernetes, for example, provides container orchestration across different environments, ensuring interoperability and smooth integration of services.

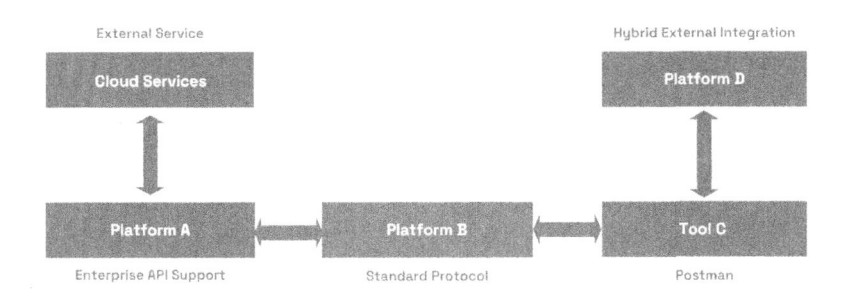

Ecosystem Enablement

Platforms should foster ecosystems where external developers, partners, and third-party services can contribute and integrate. This approach enhances the platform's value by driving innovation and expanding functionality. Samsung's Android ecosystem, supported by the Galaxy Store, is a strong example, enabling a vast array of third-party apps that enhance user engagement and contribute to the platform's success.

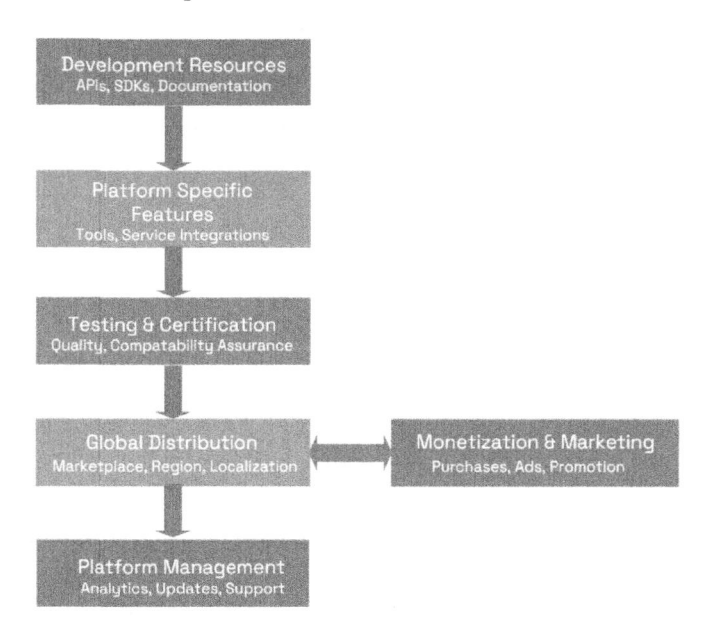

```
Development Resources
APIs, SDKs, Documentation
          │
          ▼
Platform Specific Features
Tools, Service Integrations
          │
          ▼
Testing & Certification
Quality, Compatability Assurance
          │
          ▼
Global Distribution              Monetization & Marketing
Marketplace, Region, Localization ◄──► Purchases, Ads, Promotion
          │
          ▼
Platform Management
Analytics, Updates, Support
```

User-centric design

User-centric design prioritizes the needs and experiences of platform users—whether developers, end-users, or partners—across every aspect of the architecture. A user-centric approach ensures the platform remains intuitive, accessible, and valuable, fostering adoption and loyalty. For instance, Shopify's architecture allows the backend to serve multiple frontends, such as web and mobile, exemplifying how design can be tailored to varied user experiences.

```
[Personalization] <=> [Frontend] <=> [Backend]
User Needs/Centricity    Ux/UI Design    Functionality
```

Flexibility and Adaptability

Future-proofing platforms require designing with flexibility and adaptability in mind, ensuring they can evolve alongside emerging technologies and changing market demands. This principle helps platforms remain relevant over time and reduces the need for costly overhauls. Composable platform architectures, which allow modular updates and reconfiguration without disrupting the entire system, are a good example of this principle in action.

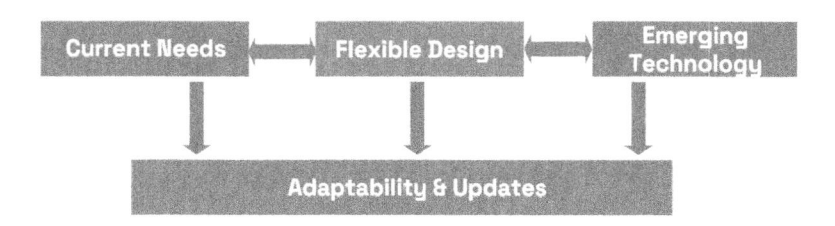

```
[Current Needs] <=> [Flexible Design] <=> [Emerging Technology]
              ↓         ↓            ↓
         [Adaptability & Updates]
```

Operational Efficiency

Platforms should be optimized for efficient operation by incorporating automated monitoring, logging, and resource management. This principle helps reduce costs, minimize downtime, and ensure the platform can maintain high performance under varying conditions. For instance, efficient data storage and management systems, such as centralized databases or distributed storage solutions, can streamline data access and persistence, making operations more efficient for both developers and users.

Automated Processes	Monitoring & Logging System	Resource Management
Internal Developer Platforms, DevOps, IaC etc.	Real-Time	Dynamic Scaling

Collaboration and Co-Creation

Fostering a collaborative environment between platform providers, orchestrators (those who manage and control the platform's operation), and complementors (third-party developers or companies that build products or services on the platform) is essential for platform success. This collaboration amplifies platform usage and strengthens network effects. By embracing this principle, platforms ensure continuous innovation, align their evolution with user needs, and leverage the strengths of all ecosystem participants. A clear example to relate this principle can be Airbnb's platform, where Airbnb (the provider and orchestrator) partners with hosts (complementors) who offer accommodations and with third-party service providers who enhance the user experience, such as cleaning services or local tour operators. This collaboration drives platform growth by expanding offerings and improving the user experience.

Platform Provider	Orchestrators	Complementors
Core Technology	Marketplace, APIs	Third Party Devs

These are key platform design principles. The more closely your platform aligns with these principles, the greater its value will be.

Platform Design Approach

In an open (or community-driven) platform architecture, such as those built on open-source projects like Kubernetes or Kafka, external developers have the freedom to build on top of the existing system, enhancing its ecosystem. This openness fosters innovation and collaboration, allowing developers to create complementary tools and services that extend the platform's functionality and make it more self-sufficient. However, the open nature can also introduce security risks and challenges in maintaining consistent quality and compatibility across contributions.

In contrast, closed (or vendor-provided) platforms, such as AWS ECS Fargate or Apple's iOS, offer a more controlled environment where the platform owner maintains stricter control over what can be developed or integrated. This approach ensures a consistent user experience and higher security but may limit the scope for external innovation.

When designing your platform, it's essential to consider which approach works best for your specific platform and its intended use.

Platform Design Elements

Design elements can vary greatly depending on your business context and level of involvement. However, there are fundamental elements and components that architects must consider while working on platform design. These major elements are crucial for every scaling platform, though there may be more specific ones tailored to your business needs. Here are the common and important ones:

Infrastructure

The role of cloud services (e.g., AWS, Azure, Google Cloud) is critical in modern platform architecture, focusing on scalability, resilience, and ease of integration. Architects can choose from various self-managed to fully managed service options to meet their specific needs.

Services/ Applications Design

Structuring services and applications to ensure they meet business requirements and can scale efficiently. While this may sometimes fall outside the platform architect's direct scope, they work closely with the business or domain teams to align on these aspects, as platforms are ultimately designed to enable business growth.

DevOps and Releases

Implementing continuous integration and continuous deployment (CI/CD) pipelines to streamline development and release processes. There are many practices, both new and established, around this, which we will delve into further in the next chapter where it belongs.

Containerization and Orchestration

Using technologies like Docker and Kubernetes to containerize applications and manage workloads efficiently. This ensures portability, scalability, and effective resource management across different environments. Orchestration tools automate the deployment, scaling, and operation of these containers, further enhancing system resilience.

API Management

Managing APIs effectively to ensure seamless communication between different services and platforms. API management tools provide security, scalability, and version control, enabling external developers and internal teams to integrate with the platform more efficiently. This is essential for fostering external innovation while maintaining control.

Packaging and Interfaces

Designing intuitive packaging and interfaces for both internal and external users, ensuring ease of use, integration, and adoption. This involves creating user-friendly interfaces for developers, businesses, and end-users, along with standardized packages that simplify onboarding and interaction with the platform.

Integrations and Interoperability

Ensuring seamless integration and interoperability of different systems and services is crucial for a platform's success. This includes user and feature management, infrastructure, networking, and other platforms. The ability to integrate diverse systems smoothly enhances flexibility, reduces silos, and facilitates a more connected ecosystem, which is essential for scaling and evolving platforms.

Security, Regulations, and Integrated Access Management

Implementing robust security measures is critical to protecting data and systems from threats, while adhering to industry regulations (such as GDPR or HIPAA) ensures compliance. Integrated access management controls allow for fine-grained access to resources. Typically, organisations establish specialised security teams, but platform architects play a crucial role in guiding these teams and aligning security strategies with the platform's broader objectives.

Data Management and Governance

Effectively managing business data is key to platform success. This involves ensuring data availability, addressing the challenges of centralization and decentralization, and mitigating issues such as silos and duplication. Domain-driven design principles can be applied to ensure the data architecture aligns with business objectives. Additionally, data governance must be established to ensure that decisions are data-driven rather than reactive, promoting strategic growth.

Measurement

Establishing clear metrics for assessing platform performance and success is essential. This includes financial assessments, monitoring spend, and evaluating user and consumer experiences. Metrics should be embedded into the platform design to ensure ongoing optimisation and improvement. We have covered more about metrics and measurement in the Platform Definition and subsequent chapters, offering a deeper dive into how they contribute to platform success.

Workflows, Standards, and Governance

Defining and maintaining workflows, standards, and governance policies is critical for ensuring consistency, security, and compliance across the platform. Effective governance covers not only technical standards but also operational workflows that streamline processes across teams and departments. The scope of governance can vary greatly, depending on the platform's usage, scale, and geographical reach. This includes defining coding standards, data privacy protocols, architectural guidelines, and process automation frameworks to ensure uniformity, adherence to best practices, and efficient operations.

Innovate and Iterate

Platforms must encourage innovation and continuous iteration to remain competitive. Decisions should be made with a time-to-live (TTL) mindset, allowing for experimentation with emerging technologies. It's important to test these technologies early in their development cycle to ensure their effectiveness before fully integrating them into the platform. This approach fosters a culture of agility and adaptation, allowing the platform to evolve as new technologies and business needs emerge.

Successful platforms often incorporate many or all of these elements. When these design elements are combined with design principles and the platform approach, as discussed in this chapter, they create a lasting legacy—provided they are implemented as planned (the focus of the next chapter).

What's Your Platform Design Like?

It's time to pause and evaluate your platform design. Is it aligned with your business model and technology stack? Consider the following scenarios to identify the design patterns you're building upon or diverging from:

- Are you operating in a B2C model using SaaS software to deliver your services?

- Is your B2C model built on a multi-stack technology aligned with hybrid cloud complexities?

- Are you operating in a complex domain such as automotive, banking, or airlines, utilising hybrid cloud and multi-decision platforms distributed globally? Which of these platforms are the most critical?

The more you narrow down your specific situation, the more effective and relatable your platform design will be. How are you performing in this aspect of your platform success blueprint? Are you doing fine, or does this need improvement? What are the areas that need the most improvement?

To manage and execute your platform effectively, you must first master its strategy and architecture, even if you later seek assistance or outsource the implementation. These critical aspects should never be outsourced or ignored. While many business functions can be delegated, your platform's core must remain under your control. The platform space is rapidly expanding, and outsourcing is rarely as efficient as in-house expertise. Invest time in understanding your platform's needs, which will allow you to collaborate effectively with external partners and ensure your platform remains robust, innovative, and aligned with your vision.

Hope you have taken some time to reflect on the importance of design and architecture in platform success; now let's dive into the popular platform design patterns and responsibilities.

Popular Platform Design Patterns

The three types of platforms mentioned earlier in this chapter (business, external enablement, internal enablement) can be built using various architectural patterns, each offering specific benefits depending on the platform's needs and objectives. Here's a closer look at some of the key architectural patterns and examples of their application. While this is by no means a complete list, it provides a solid understanding of the most widely used architectural patterns. In most practical situations, you will find that more than one pattern is used to realise a platform.

Headless Platform Architecture

In a headless architecture, the platform's back end is decoupled from its front end, allowing the back end to serve different frontends through APIs. For example, **Shopify** uses a headless architecture where the same backend supports multiple interfaces, such as web, mobile, and IoT, enabling flexibility in how content and services are delivered to users.

Ecosystem Platform Architecture

This pattern focuses on building a platform that integrates with other platforms, third-party services, and APIs, creating an ecosystem where multiple participants can contribute and extend the platform's capabilities. External enablement platforms often use this pattern to manage the ecosystem users and partners. For example, **Samsung** or **Apple's** application stores platform enables third-party developers to create apps that expand the platform's functionality, fostering a rich ecosystem of complementary products and services.

Composable Platform Architecture

A composable platform architecture allows for modular components to be assembled and reassembled into different configurations to meet specific user needs or use cases. For example, **Adobe Experience Manager (AEM)** uses composable architecture to allow businesses to create tailored digital experiences by combining content management, e-commerce, and personalization modules in different ways to suit their specific requirements. This approach involves selecting reusable components and integrating them to form a platform.

Repository Platform Architecture

This pattern is used to manage data access and persistence. It abstracts the logic needed to access data stored in databases or other data sources, making it easier to manage and test. Internal Enablement Platforms often use the repository pattern to streamline data management for developers. For example, **GitHub** uses the repository pattern to manage code repositories, allowing developers to efficiently retrieve, manipulate, and maintain version control across large-scale projects.

Layered Architecture

This pattern organizes the platform into distinct layers, each with specific responsibilities, such as presentation, business logic, and data access. A classic example is enterprise applications where the user interface, business rules, and data management are separated.

Business platform architecture often employs this pattern to manage complexity, ensuring that each layer can be developed, tested, and maintained independently. For instance, **Amazon** utilizes layered architecture in its **Amazon.com e**-commerce Platform to separate user interface, business logic, and data management layers, enabling efficient scaling and maintenance of its vast e-commerce operations.

Event-Driven Architecture

In this pattern, systems react to events generated by other systems or components. It's particularly effective for cases such as external enablement platforms where real-time processing and responsiveness are essential. A common use case is in microservices architectures for handling events like order processing in an online shopping platform. Additionally, IoT platforms might use event-driven architecture to manage and respond to data from connected devices. **Netflix** relies on event-driven architecture within its **Netflix Streaming Platform** to manage its microservices, ensuring that user interactions, like playing a video, trigger real-time responses across its global service.

Microservices Platform Architecture

This architectural pattern divides platform functionality into smaller, independently deployable services, each responsible for a specific business function. This approach is ideal for platforms that need to scale and evolve rapidly. For example, **Netflix** employs a microservices architecture to manage various functions such as user management, content streaming, and recommendation algorithms. Each service operates independently, allowing for isolated development, deployment, and scaling, which significantly enhances the platform's flexibility and fault tolerance. Furthermore, container orchestration tools like **Kubernetes** help manage and deploy these microservices efficiently. Services like **Istio** facilitate communication between microservices while adding essential features such as load balancing, traffic management, and security, ensuring a robust and scalable platform.

Hexagonal Architecture (Ports and Adapters)

This pattern is designed to make a platform more maintainable and adaptable to change. It's particularly well-suited for API Management Platforms where the core business logic is decoupled from the delivery mechanisms, allowing for easy integration with different clients (e.g., web apps, mobile apps). This architecture is also valuable in cases such as Payment Processing Systems, where different payment gateways can be plugged in without altering the core logic. For example, **Adyen**, a global payments platform, uses a hexagonal architecture to integrate multiple payment methods without affecting its core processing logic, ensuring adaptability and ease of maintenance.

API Gateway Architecture

An API Gateway sits at the front of a platform, routing requests to appropriate backend services or microservices, providing a unified entry point for external clients. For example, a multi-tenant SaaS platform might use an API Gateway to manage requests from different tenants, handle authentication, rate limiting, and direct traffic to the appropriate services. **Amazon Web Services (AWS)** uses an API Gateway in its cloud services to manage and scale incoming API requests efficiently, providing a unified and secure entry point for different services.

Platform as a Service (PaaS) Architecture

In PaaS architecture, the platform provides a complete development and deployment environment in the cloud, abstracting infrastructure complexities from users. For example, **Google App Engine** and **AWS Elastic Beanstalk** allow developers to deploy applications without worrying about the underlying infrastructure, enabling rapid development and scaling of applications.

Multi-Tenant Architecture

This pattern involves designing the platform so that multiple tenants (users or organizations) share the same instance of software while keeping their data and configurations isolated. For example, **Salesforce** uses multi-tenant architecture to serve different customers from a single software instance, allowing for efficient resource usage and simplified maintenance while ensuring data isolation between tenants.

Who is responsible for platform design and architecture?

Platform design and architecture are typically managed by individuals or teams with a strong understanding of technology and how it can be applied to solve business challenges. These professionals are often referred to as Platform Architects, Architects, or similar titles. Their main responsibility is to ensure the platform is designed to meet current needs while also being scalable and adaptable for the future.

To succeed in this role, Platform Architects must have a solid grasp of platform strategy (Chapter 7), platform experience and economization (Chapter 8), and technology strategy (Chapter 9). Additionally, they need expertise in system architecture, integration, and emerging technologies to create a robust platform that can grow with the business.

Along with these responsibilities, Platform Architects work closely with teams to make sure the platform development follows the intended design. They play a crucial role in ensuring that platform strategy, user experience, and technical execution all align seamlessly. Moreover, their involvement helps keep the platform innovative, responsive to feedback, and aligned with the evolving needs of the business.

Common Design & Architecture Pitfalls

There are several pitfalls that organisations face when designing platforms. Here are five of the most common:

1. **Startup Mindset Design**:
    Teams often focus on rapid iteration through MVPs and prototypes without laying a solid design foundation. This can lead to systems, integration challenges, inefficient use

of resources, poor user experience, and difficulties transitioning to production-ready systems.

2. **Reactive Design and Architecture**:
Without a proper strategic plan, teams react to issues as they arise, leading to resource inefficiencies, inconsistent architecture, integration problems, performance bottlenecks, and a lack of automation. A proactive design approach with unified architecture and automation can prevent these issues.

3. **Disconnected Design from Implementation**:
Even with a strong design, if it isn't effectively communicated, it can fail in execution. Misalignment between design and development processes leads to inefficiencies, wasted resources, and a final product that doesn't meet the intended goals. Clear communication and alignment between teams are essential to bridge this gap.

4. **Growth and Sustainability Challenges**:
Platforms often struggle to scale due to poor initial design or resource constraints. Decisions that worked at the beginning may not scale as the platform grows. Integrating legacy systems and prioritising short-term fixes over long-term sustainability further complicates scalability. Regularly re-evaluating design decisions and planning for future growth are key to overcoming these challenges.

5. **Other Common Design Challenges**:
Key issues include technical debt, lack of long-term planning, poor documentation, and security vulnerabilities.

Organisations often fail by not empowering architects or giving them authority to align teams with the right strategy. Additionally, focusing on quick fixes instead of addressing the root causes of problems leads to greater challenges over time.

Addressing these pitfalls requires a combination of strategic foresight, clear communication, and empowering architects to ensure cohesive platform design and development.

Where to start?

Whether you're starting from scratch or somewhere along your platform journey, you can follow these steps and tailor them to your specific platform needs. The key is to be intentional about platform design and architecture:

1. List your platform(s) and assess their criticality.

2. Begin with the most critical platform and involve a platform architect throughout the process.

3. Assess the current design and document the "As-Is" state if it's not already documented. If you're starting fresh, this serves as an essential guide to avoid falling into the trap of multi-year refinements.

4. Choose the architecture pattern that best fits your platform's needs, considering some of the popular patterns discussed earlier.

5. Identify any gaps or overlooked aspects in the design, particularly in relation to your platform and technology strategy. Consider long-term factors and key principles such as scalability, cost, and regulatory requirements.

6. Create an iterative plan, prioritising key action items.

7. Document decisions and the new "To-Be" design, ensuring it's integrated into your platform roadmap.

8. Communicate regularly with platform development teams and other stakeholders.

9. Ensure the design is understood and implemented correctly (discussed in detail in Chapter 11).

10. Measure progress and iterate at a pre-set frequency.

To summarize: Proactively tackling platform design and architecture requires a strategic approach that focuses on building a cohesive system architecture, efficiently allocating resources, and delivering a consistent, high-quality user experience. The steps outlined in this chapter guide platform architects through assessing platform needs, documenting current designs, and implementing architecture patterns suited to long-term scalability, cost, and compliance. Key elements such as identifying gaps, integrating decisions into roadmaps, and fostering continuous communication with stakeholders are crucial. This forms the foundation for effective platform management and ensures a well-designed system that can adapt to evolving demands.

As I quoted at the beginning of this chapter, "Building a platform takes effort, right? That's why it's worth investing the time to design it right!" With a strong architectural base established, this is a logical point to transition into the next phase of platform development and engineering, where we will explore implementation in greater detail.

Key Takeaways:

- Aligning platform and technology strategies is crucial for driving purposeful design and architecture. When tailored to fit your business model, this alignment can be a game changer.

- Understand your platform type—whether it's a business, external, or internal platform—to guide your design and strategy effectively.

- Involve a Platform Architect and assign the right responsibilities to avoid common problem patterns, as discussed earlier.

- Choose a platform architecture pattern that complements both your platform and technology strategies.

- There's no specific time to start integrating the right design and architecture principles—begin at any stage using the steps provided as a guideline.

Chapter Eleven

Platform Development To Operations

"Never wrestle with a technology problem; break it into manageable pieces and conquer it step by step."

Building a platform is just the beginning. The real challenge—and opportunity—lies in the journey from development to operations. This transition is where your platform truly comes to life, delivering value to users and generating business impact. In this chapter, we'll explore the critical steps and strategies needed to ensure a smooth and successful transition from platform development to ongoing operations. We'll discuss aligning development practices with operational requirements, the importance of automation, and the role of continuous monitoring and improvement in maintaining a high-performing platform.

Platform development involves leveraging tools to develop, test, deploy, and monitor features, ensuring users can interact effectively. This approach requires continuous updates to enhance platform capabilities and scalability. The development stage becomes seamless when built on the artefacts produced in earlier stages of the Platform Success Blueprint, particularly platform design and architecture. With a strong foundation, development becomes more straightforward, as most technology and platform strategy challenges are addressed upfront, and design is aligned with known constraints and requirements. For instance, having a clear direction on what features to develop, which tools to use, what integrations and interfaces to employ, and which security and regulatory aspects to adhere to makes development smoother.

If you haven't read Chapters 9 and 10 yet, I highly recommend doing so to understand the crucial differences between platform design and platform development.

DECODING PLATFORM PATTERNS

In the platform world, some companies are getting it right, while many others struggle. You can assess your platform development practices by reflecting on these questions:

- How is the experience for your engineering teams?

- How quickly can they move things to production? (For instance, if developers can start developing in seconds or minutes, that's a good sign; if it takes days or weeks, that's concerning.)

- How much support is needed for your platforms?

- Do security and compliance regulations take significant effort to get features to production?

- Are people familiar with your platforms, or do they struggle to use them?

- Do they get or maintain well-written design and architecture documents?

- Another classic problem is whether you are genuinely building and serving a platform—or a myth (discussed in Chapter 3).

These indicators can highlight your platform practices and pain points. If any of these areas are weak, it might suggest that your culture and processes need attention, or that there's too much (or too little) being built into the platform due to a lack of design and architecture. Communication about platform strategy and design might also be uncoordinated, leading to an overloaded development stage, which puts stress on the development cycle and teams.

Platform providers and builders of any scale face numerous challenges today, many of which fall into one or more of the categories mentioned above. We will discuss the most prominent challenges and potential solutions in this chapter.

This chapter is positioned here for a reason—while there's a lot of buzz around platform engineering, this book aims to cut through the hype and offer a comprehensive view and practical blueprint for platform success, without promising something unachievable, but delivering lasting value. By understanding the aspects covered in previous chapters and assessing your current ways of working, the development side of things becomes easier, which is the ultimate goal of this Platform Success Blueprint.

Platform Development vs. Software Development

Let's use a simple analogy to explain the concept of a container (laptop) and its content (software apps).

If software development is like creating a specific software application, then platform development is like designing and maintaining a laptop (or engine) that can run any number of applications. Software development focuses on the tools and creativity needed to solve a particular task—whether that's writing a report, editing a video, or building a new app. Each task is designed for a specific need.

In contrast, platform development is about ensuring that the laptop (platform) is powerful, well-organized, and equipped with the necessary hardware and operating system to support any type of software. It's about creating an environment where any user can turn it on, find the applications they need, and start working right away. The platform (laptop) provides the stability, consistency, and resources needed to run multiple software applications smoothly, enabling continuous productivity and innovation.

Referring back to the platform definition from Chapter 4, a platform serves its true purpose when it provides stability and clear interfaces. By viewing the platform as the laptop and software development as the various activities and applications running on it, you can better understand how each component fits into the larger picture. This technology analogy highlights the distinction and importance of platform development.

When considering the three prominent types of platforms discussed in Chapter 10—Business Platforms (for end-users), External Enablement Platforms (for the business ecosystem and network effects), and Internal Enablement Platforms (for in-house use)—platform development should be approached similarly across all types. The differences lie in the complexity and criticality, which vary based on the level of automation, user experience, and features.

Platform development involves software engineering practices, but its purpose—to create an encapsulation of services that serve many other common or related purposes with time —makes it distinct from software development. This distinction brings more complexity and preparation, ensuring the platform can support various software and innovations effectively.

Platform development is a comprehensive process that encompasses everything from end-to-end development to ongoing operations. It involves multiple critical steps, which we will delve into shortly. However, it's crucial first to identify and understand the common challenges in this process. Addressing these challenges upfront will make the subsequent solutions and remaining elements of platform development clearer and more manageable.

Platform Development - Challenges

- **Technology Variety:** Managing diverse technologies within the platform.

- **Technology Changes:** Adapting to rapid technological advancements.

- **Fragmented Technology:** Dealing with incompatible systems and solutions.

- **DevOps:** Implementing efficient DevOps practices.

- **Hybrid Infrastructure (Cloud) Complexities:** Managing network, security, data, and standards across hybrid cloud environments.

- **Technology Learning Curve:** Ensuring the team is skilled in the latest technologies.

To reinforce this point: Major decisions—whether related to technology, complexity, or user experience—should not be offloaded onto the development phase. Each stage requires specific expertise and a well-thought-out plan and roadmap, which should be established before reaching development. This was discussed in the previous chapter on platform design and architecture, where we identified a significant issue: architects failing to effectively communicate design expectations and standards to implementation teams or being preoccupied with tasks other than platform design.

If you've recognized this as a gap in your process, don't place the burden on platform engineers, developers, and SREs. Instead, take the time to address it properly by applying the processes and techniques discussed in previous chapters. Revisit your platform strategy, ensure it's reflected at the design level, and then hand it off to the development team to follow the established path. When handled properly, most of the challenges mentioned above will be managed, leaving only a few for the development stage. In this chapter, we'll focus on those specific challenges relevant to platform development.

Platform development can be overwhelming, requiring careful consideration of several aspects. For example, the sheer number of tools, partially exposed platforms, and integration features create a challenging environment for maintaining and developing at pace. With the rise of open-source solutions and cloud-native technologies becoming the norm, cloud providers offer service models tailored to specific tasks, but it's up to you to orchestrate both new and existing systems. This responsibility places a heavy burden on platform engineers, who must manage everything from infrastructure setup to continuous monitoring.

Consider the dependency ecosystem and the dispersed nature of systems like Kubernetes, a widely adopted open-source project for container orchestration and lifecycle management.

DECODING PLATFORM PATTERNS

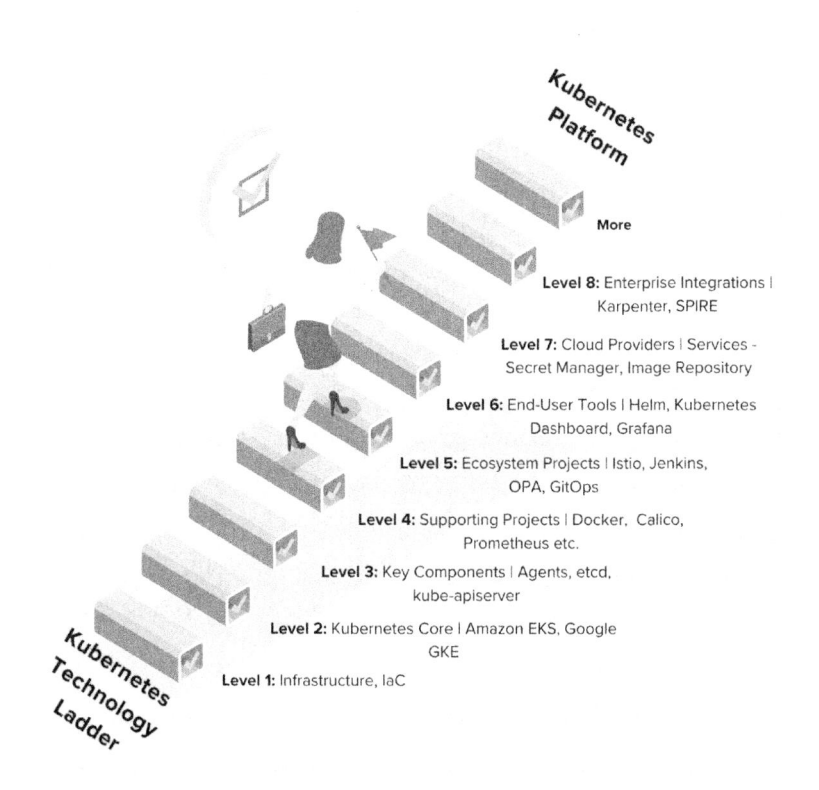

Kubernetes Platform

More

Level 8: Enterprise Integrations | Karpenter, SPIRE

Level 7: Cloud Providers | Services - Secret Manager, Image Repository

Level 6: End-User Tools | Helm, Kubernetes Dashboard, Grafana

Level 5: Ecosystem Projects | Istio, Jenkins, OPA, GitOps

Level 4: Supporting Projects | Docker, Calico, Prometheus etc.

Level 3: Key Components | Agents, etcd, kube-apiserver

Level 2: Kubernetes Core | Amazon EKS, Google GKE

Level 1: Infrastructure, IaC

Kubernetes Technology Ladder

Kubernetes has become the go-to solution for developing microservices and cloud-native architectures. It's a revolutionary container orchestration mechanism that has standardized tasks like cluster formation and work orchestration through containers—previously separate efforts for each company. However, this has created a complex chain of dependencies. To utilize Kubernetes effectively, developers must integrate an entire suite of dependencies, spanning from Level 1 to Level 8, as shown in the diagram, and beyond. Even though cloud providers like AWS (with EKS) and GCP (with GKE) offer integrated features, many components still need to be integrated separately to transform Kubernetes into a fully-fledged platform for developing business services.

Moreover, all these layers, from Level 1 to Level 8, are in constant flux, meaning any change in one layer can trigger a ripple effect throughout the entire stack. These changes happen so frequently that they cannot be ignored or avoided. This dynamic environment makes it increasingly challenging to maintain development speed and drive innovation, despite the integration of many AI-assisted tools designed to make development easier.

This is just one example, but it highlights the granularity and complexity involved in platform development. These are the kinds of technology challenges that platform developers and engineers are currently grappling with.

Every platform company faces these challenges, with some reporting a major increase in the number of engineers required to complete development work and realize the platform compared to earlier stages. This significantly increases the burden on organizations, forcing them to either purchase comprehensive solutions that bundle these capabilities or undertake the work themselves for better control and future evolution. For reasons like these, there is a growing need for internal platforms that can manage and mitigate these complexities.

What are the Solutions or Solution Patterns?

Is there a solution to the platform development challenges mentioned above? While there are emerging approaches, they are still in the process of maturing. I have stated and reinforced in the past and will do so again (read here https://pandainnovators.com/is-kubernetes-and-ecosystem-boring-or-boon/), that it's in everyone's best interest to address the fragmented technology ecosystem with more integrated and affordable solutions. In the meantime, organizations should focus on building strong platform development practices, streamlining and refining the responsibilities of engineers, and taking internal development platforms seriously.

Let's explore the patterns that these solutions entail.

Internal Platforms

Internal platforms are a powerful way to create bespoke solutions tailored specifically for your organization, especially when external solutions are not feasible, available, or aligned with your unique requirements. These platforms can take various forms, such as custom test automation frameworks to streamline testing processes, internal development platforms that unify and optimize the development environment, or specialized automation tools designed to address specific operational challenges. By developing these custom platforms, organizations can achieve greater control, flexibility, and efficiency, ensuring their internal processes align precisely with strategic goals and operational needs.

Internal Developer Platforms (IDPs)

The concept of Internal Developer Platforms (IDPs) is rapidly gaining traction across various industries. IDPs are internal platforms designed to revolutionize development and operations by streamlining processes and significantly improving efficiency. By providing developers with a cohesive set of integrated, automated, and well-orchestrated tools and systems, IDPs empower teams to focus on building innovative solutions, minimizing the friction and complexity often associated with development workflows.

IDPs are becoming increasingly popular due to the complexities involved in integrating, building, and customizing cloud-native platforms, automating infrastructure operations, and enhancing self-service workflows for developers. As seen in the example of setting up a complete Kubernetes platform, requires a more holistic approach, where automation through platforms becomes essential. IDPs extend DevOps culture by embedding practices from infrastructure to operations and integrating organization-specific processes or workflows into the platform. The ultimate goal is to build robust internal platforms that can be leveraged to accelerate the development of internal, business, and external platforms.

IDPs aim to create a seamless, end-to-end environment that encompasses all aspects of the development lifecycle—ranging from infrastructure services and coding to testing, deployment, monitoring and more—ensuring that every component is connected and optimized for maximum productivity. By integrating these elements into a single, unified platform, IDPs enhance developer productivity, promote consistency, reduce errors, and accelerate the delivery of high-quality software. Additionally, they increase the pace at which you can support other business and external platforms.

Setting up an ideal IDP presents numerous challenges due to the many moving parts involved, with constantly upgrading technologies and individually changing components. On top of that, every company's dynamics—such as processes, culture, and workflows—are different, making the task even more complex. It's akin to continuously repairing and extending the foundation of a ship while it's sailing (more on this in Chapter 13).

Core Components of an IDP

To effectively set up an Internal Developer Platform (IDP), it's essential to understand its core components and how they contribute to the overall development and operational process.

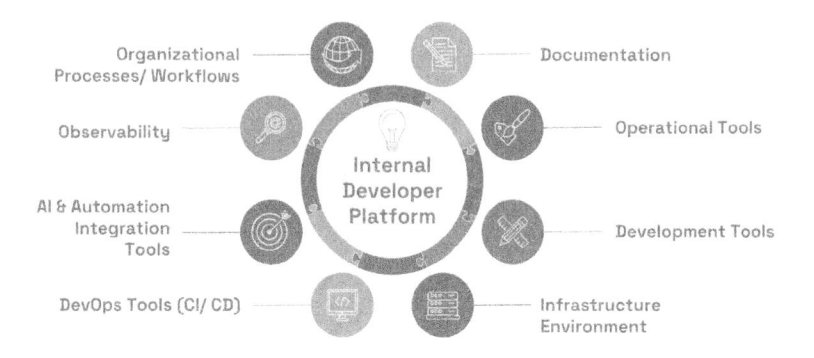

Diagram: Internal Developer Platform surrounded by — Organizational Processes/Workflows, Documentation, Observability, Operational Tools, AI & Automation Integration Tools, Development Tools, DevOps Tools (CI/CD), Infrastructure Environment.

An IDP consists of various elements that work together to streamline the development and management of platforms, each playing a distinct role in enabling efficient workflows and scalability:

- **Infrastructure Environment**: This is the foundation where platform applications run, providing the necessary resources for scaling and flexibility. In the platform context, cloud platforms and container orchestration systems ensure seamless operation across diverse environments. Examples include AWS, GCP, Azure services, Kubernetes, and Docker.

- **Development Tools**: These tools support core development activities such as coding, version control, and automated testing, ensuring that developers can build and iterate rapidly within the platform. For platform development, these tools help teams collaborate efficiently and maintain consistent code quality. Common examples are Git, GitHub, GitLab, Jenkins, Visual Studio Code, and IntelliJ.

- **Operation Toolchain**: This set of tools manages platform deployments and scaling while ensuring reliability. It plays a crucial role in keeping the platform operational and responsive, reducing downtime and enabling smooth updates. Examples include Terraform, Ansible, and Helm.

- **Continuous Deployment Tools**: These tools automate the deployment pipeline, ensuring rapid and reliable delivery of applications across different environments. In the platform context, they help maintain agility while ensuring stable and continuous updates. Popular tools include Jenkins, CircleCI, GitLab CI, and ArgoCD.

- **Observability**: Observability tools monitor platform performance and availability, helping to identify and resolve issues before they affect users. They provide critical insights into how well the platform operates under various conditions. Examples include Prometheus, Grafana, the ELK Stack (Elasticsearch, Logstash, Kibana), and Jaeger.

- **AI and Automation**: AI-driven tools and automation frameworks optimize workflows by handling repetitive tasks, improving development speed, and operational efficiency. In platform development, they enhance capabilities such as automated scaling, monitoring, and predictive analytics. This includes tools for code generation, testing frameworks, machine learning models for predictive analytics, Ansible Automations, and AIOps.

- **Organizational Processes Implemented as Workflows**: These tools automate and enforce organizational processes, ensuring consistent practices and smooth platform operation. In a platform context, they streamline operations such as request management and communication workflows across development teams. Examples include Jira, ServiceNow, Confluence, Slack integrations, and security tools.

- **Documentation**: Centralized platforms for creating, managing, and sharing documentation are essential for onboarding and continuous knowledge sharing across platform teams. In platform development, this documentation ensures all stakeholders are aligned and informed. Common tools include Confluence, Notion, GitHub, and Wiki.

IDPs are still in their early stages, gaining momentum thanks to open-source projects like Backstage and Kratix. Despite this progress, there is much to learn to simplify platform development for companies. Two key aspects are crucial for IDP success: first, avoiding the complication of shifting too many responsibilities onto developers, and second, measuring developer acceptance and adoption as the true indicators of success. Educating developers about the platform is essential to gain their buy-in and trust in the underlying automation. While the pattern of IDP adoption is correct, managing these aspects at an enterprise level and achieving organizational consensus remains a significant challenge.

Similarly, other internal platforms can be established to streamline various aspects of platform development, such as those dedicated to testing frameworks and automation, user experience frameworks and automation, or data pipeline management. These components broadly encompass the internal platform spectrum. The detailed examples and components of IDPs presented above should provide a clear understanding of how these internal platforms add value by speeding up the overall platform development work.

APIs (Application Programming Interfaces)

APIs are another foundational pattern that, while not new, remains crucial in modern software development. APIs provide a powerful way to ensure that interfaces are highly available, standardized, and abstracted from the underlying implementation details. They are essential for enabling composable architectures, allowing different components of a system to interact seamlessly, regardless of the underlying technology stack. This approach aligns perfectly with cloud-native features and other popular design methodologies we've discussed in previous chapters.

In my experience working for a large European bank, I observed that APIs offer an excellent method for abstracting implementation details, making it easier to develop and maintain complex systems. However, the real challenge at the enterprise scale wasn't just in implementing APIs but in ensuring their adoption and treating them with the same rigour as other software systems. This means focusing on integration, efficiency, and consistent management across the organization, rather than managing APIs in isolation. Successfully doing so requires a shift in mindset—viewing APIs not merely as connectors, but as integral components of a larger, cohesive system that drives business value. This holistic approach to API management is critical to achieving scalability, flexibility, and long-term success in any large enterprise.

Where to Start?

Platform development requires careful planning, strategic foresight, and disciplined execution. To build a truly resilient and scalable foundation for your platform, its strength must lie in a well-crafted technology strategy, coupled with robust design and architecture. These elements serve as the bedrock upon which your platform is constructed. When executed effectively, they ensure that your platform functions smoothly and efficiently, allowing you to focus on innovation and growth rather than getting bogged down by endless decisions and technical hurdles.

A strong foundation simplifies the development process and transforms your internal development practices from mere automation into fully-fledged platforms. This evolution can lead to significant gains in productivity, scalability, and business agility. Here are the steps to ensure your platform development is on the right path:

1. **Define and Follow a Clear Technology Strategy**: Establish a comprehensive technology strategy that aligns with your business goals. As discussed in Chapter 9, this strategy should ideally have been established earlier. If it's not in place, now is the time to define one. Consider current and future needs, platform strategy, technological trends, and the competitive landscape. This strategy will guide your decisions on tools, technologies, and

frameworks. Keep in mind that the more technology you introduce, the more maintenance it requires. Therefore, technology decisions should be made thoughtfully and not hastily.

2. **Design Thoughtfully**: Invest time in designing your platform with flexibility and scalability in mind. This task should not be deferred until development. Revisit Chapter 10 if necessary, and ensure these design decisions are made by platform architects or experts, then followed by developers and engineers. Consider the user experience, integration points, and how different components will interact. A well-thought-out design will minimize future rework and ensure your platform can adapt to changing requirements.

3. **Architect for the Long Term**: Develop a robust architecture that can support your platform's growth. Choose the right architectural patterns, and ensure modularity and design for maintainability and performance. A strong architecture is the backbone of a successful platform, enabling it to scale without compromising stability.

4. **Implement with Precision**: Once the strategy, design, and architecture are in place, focus on precise implementation and development. This is where the platform success blueprint comes to life. Follow best practices in coding, testing, and deployment to ensure the platform is built correctly from the ground up.

5. **Automate Where Possible**: Start by automating your

processes, workflows, and repetitive tasks within your development operations. As automation becomes more sophisticated, transition these practices into platform services or Internal Developer Platforms (IDPs) that can be reused across the organization. This shift will improve efficiency and consistency, enabling your organization to scale with less hassle and greater technology adoption.

6. **Focus on Continuous Improvement**: Platform development doesn't end with the first release. Continuously monitor performance, gather feedback, and make iterative improvements. This ongoing process will keep your platform relevant and robust, allowing it to evolve with your business needs.

7. **Educate and Empower Your Teams**: Ensure that your development teams are well-versed in the platform's design and architecture principles. Business units and ecosystem users should also be informed about changes and how to leverage the developed platforms. Provide training and resources to help them understand the platform's vision and how to use it effectively. Empowering your teams will lead to better alignment and a more cohesive development process.

By following these steps, you can build a strong foundation that supports current development needs and positions your platform for future success. This strategic approach will help you avoid the pitfalls of poorly planned development and ensure that your platform remains a powerful engine for innovation and business growth.

Key Takeaways

- Define your technology strategy early, aligning it with business goals for long-term success.

- Design for scalability, ensuring flexibility to adapt to future needs.

- Build a strong, flexible architecture to support growth and stability.

- Automate processes to enhance efficiency and enable scalable growth.

- Continuously monitor and refine your platform to stay aligned with evolving requirements.

- Empower your teams with a deep understanding of platform design and architecture principles for effective execution.

Section D

Building Legacy Through Platforms

Chapter Twelve

Mapping the User's Journey on the Platform

"Platform user's journey shines through platform experience; keep it relevant."

In the last two sections, we've delved deeply into platform concepts and the entire essential spectrum, covering everything from strategic planning to the intricate details of platform design and development. We've also addressed challenges and solutions at every stage. This chapter focuses on weaving together the ideal journeys of Platform Users (covered here) and Providers (discussed in the next chapter). These journeys will help readers map their own experiences to the six-sided Platform Success Blueprint (chapter 5), identifying areas that may need more attention.

The journeys of platform users and providers differ significantly in complexity, responsibility, impact, and continuity, making it essential to address them separately.

For platform users, the relationship with a platform begins the moment they decide to explore it and ends when they decide to move on. The platform lifecycle from a user's perspective mirrors a journey through the phases of Introduction, Navigation, and Retention. Initially, users experience discovery and enthusiasm in the introductory phase. As they become more familiar, they navigate the complexities and learning curves, gradually mastering the platform. Over time, this journey deepens into committed engagement, leading to retention—or separation if the platform no longer meets their needs. This journey requires adaptability, patience, and active participation, fostering a fulfilling and symbiotic relationship between the user and the platform.

We will now dive into each of these stages, exploring the unique challenges and recommendations at every step. Take some time to understand these challenges and advice, as they are often not communicated by platform providers. It is usually left to users to discover these issues on their own, which can affect their efforts in unexpected ways. By proactively understanding these challenges at all stages of platform usage, you can save time and focus on what truly matters, cutting down a multi-year journey to the essentials.

Introductory Phase

This is the initial phase where a user first encounters the platform. This period is marked by excitement and exploration. Users evaluate the platform's features and potential value figuring out and assessing compatibility. Platforms aim to capture interest by offering user-friendly interfaces, engaging content, and attractive incentives. First impressions are crucial here, as they determine whether the user will move forward or lose interest.

Introductory phase comprises of 3 major sub-stages:

(a) **Interest and Need Alignment:** In this initial stage, the user identifies a need or interest that aligns with the platform's offerings.

Here are some common challenges, key lessons, and advice to keep in mind and benefit from at this stage:

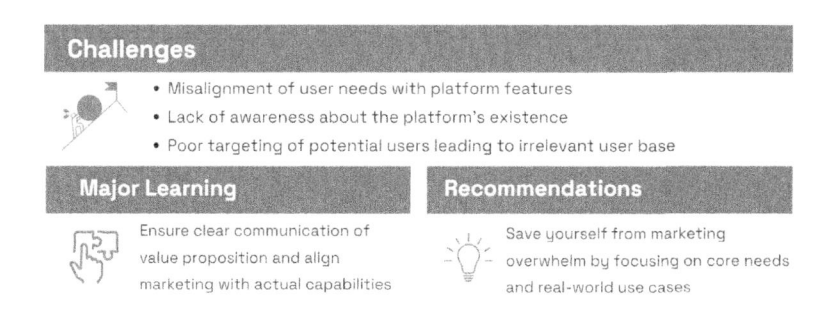

Challenges
- Misalignment of user needs with platform features
- Lack of awareness about the platform's existence
- Poor targeting of potential users leading to irrelevant user base

Major Learning
Ensure clear communication of value proposition and align marketing with actual capabilities

Recommendations
Save yourself from marketing overwhelm by focusing on core needs and real-world use cases

(b) **Evaluation:** The user evaluates the platform to see if it meets their specific needs. This involves exploring its features, reading reviews, and possibly utilizing introductory offers.

Here are some common challenges, key lessons, and advice to keep in mind and benefit from at this stage:

Challenges
- Overwhelming options and information
- Difficulty in comparing with competitors
- Lack of detailed technical specifications or documentation for evaluation

Major Learning
Detailed and transparent evaluation criteria can prevent missteps

Recommendations
Do thorough research, seek unbiased reviews, and prioritize hands-on trials

(c) **Onboarding:** If the platform meets the user's needs, they move on to the onboarding process. This involves setting up an account, customizing preferences, and familiarizing themselves with the platform.

Here are some common challenges, key lessons, and advice to keep in mind and benefit from at this stage:

Challenges
- Complex account setup process
- Insufficient onboarding support and tutorials
- Poor data import/export capabilities
- Lack of integration with identity management systems

Major Learning
Effective onboarding is crucial for long-term user engagement

Recommendations
Provide comprehensive onboarding materials, tutorials, and proactive customer support

In the **Introductory Phase**, aligning the user's needs with the platform's capabilities, thoroughly evaluating the platform, and ensuring a smooth onboarding process are vital steps. These foundational actions significantly influence the user's ongoing experience and their decision to continue using the platform.

Navigation Phase

If the Introduction phase is successful, the user transitions into the Navigation phase, where they engage with the platform at a deeper level. During this phase, the user begins to integrate the platform into their daily routine or as per requirement, relying on it for essential functions and consistently utilizing its features.

This phase often presents challenges such as technical issues, usability problems, and the need for effective integrations and interfaces. As users become more proficient, they start unlocking the platform's full potential. For platforms, this is a critical stage for building trust and loyalty through excellent customer support, continuous updates, and fostering a sense of community.

The Navigation phase consists of three sub-stages: integrate, run, or drop. In some cases, users may drop if their interests do not align at the usage level or if the platform experience falls short.

(a) **Integrate:** Once onboarded, the user integrates the platform into their routine usage. They rely on it for essential functions and continuously engage with its features.

Here are some common challenges, key lessons, and advice to keep in mind and benefit from at this stage:

Challenges

- Difficulty integrating with existing systems and tools
- Compatibility issues or limited customization options to meet specific business needs
- Inconsistent data synchronization with other platforms
- Security vulnerabilities during integration

Major Learning

Proper planning and evaluation of integration points are essential

Recommendations

Check integration points well in advance for better compatibility with existing systems

(b) **Run:** The user relies on the platform for regular activities, experiencing both the benefits and challenges of its continuous use.

Here are some common challenges, key lessons, and advice to keep in mind and benefit from at this stage:

Challenges

- Steep learning curve for users
- Frequent technical issues or bugs
- Poor user interface design
- Scalability issues as user base grows
- Data latency and performance issues
- Difficulty in tracking and managing user permissions and roles

Major Learning

Continuous support and user feedback loops can enhance user experience and platform reliability

Recommendations

Do not be too early to assume that integration is not going to work; be patient and thorough

(c) **Drop (Gradually or Decisively Part Ways):** Not all users will remain engaged. Some may encounter issues or find better alternatives, leading them to gradually reduce usage or decisively switch platforms. At this point, the platform's network effects and overall user experience play a critical role in either retaining users or causing them to lose interest and disengage. Numerous social media examples, both successful and failed attempts, discussed earlier in this book serve as prime examples of this dynamic.

Here are some common challenges, key lessons, and advice to keep in mind and benefit from at this stage:

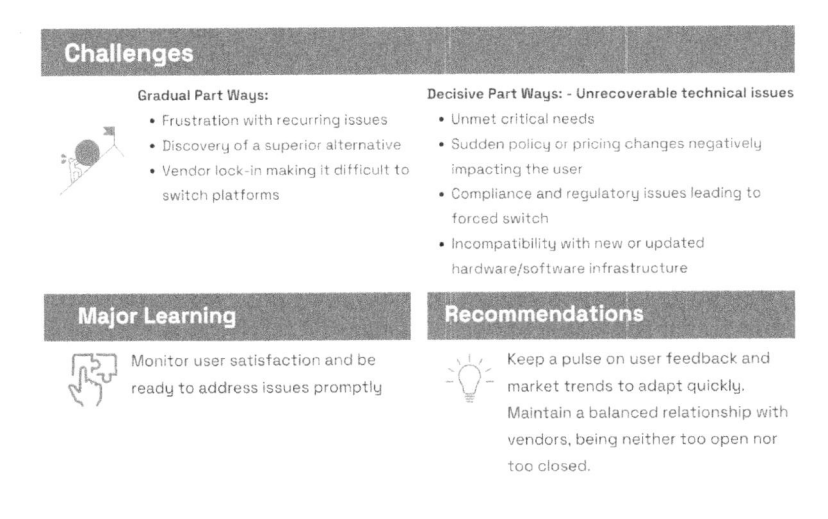

Challenges

Gradual Part Ways:
- Frustration with recurring issues
- Discovery of a superior alternative
- Vendor lock-in making it difficult to switch platforms

Decisive Part Ways: - Unrecoverable technical issues
- Unmet critical needs
- Sudden policy or pricing changes negatively impacting the user
- Compliance and regulatory issues leading to forced switch
- Incompatibility with new or updated hardware/software infrastructure

Major Learning

Monitor user satisfaction and be ready to address issues promptly

Recommendations

Keep a pulse on user feedback and market trends to adapt quickly. Maintain a balanced relationship with vendors, being neither too open nor too closed.

Retention Phase

The Retention phase represents a mature and enduring relationship between the user and the platform. By this stage, users are deeply integrated into the platform's ecosystem, often evolving into advocates or loyal supporters. This phase is marked by stability and mutual benefit, with users being well-versed in the platform's features and feeling a strong sense of belonging within the community.

The platform, in turn, continues to evolve, introducing new features and improvements to keep users engaged and invested. This ongoing innovation helps maintain user interest and reinforces their commitment to the platform.

(a) **Maintain:** Users who continue with the platform enter the maintenance phase, where they regularly update their usage practices, apply version upgrades, and keep the platform integrated into their workflow.

Here are some common challenges, key lessons, and advice to keep in mind and benefit from at this stage:

Challenges
- Need for regular updates and maintenance
- Risk of platform obsolescence
- Continuous monitoring for security vulnerabilities
- Increased complexity in managing and maintaining the platform as it evolves
- Dependency on third-party plugins or extensions that may become unsupported

Major Learning
Proactive maintenance and updates are key to platform longevity

Recommendations
Stay current with updates and best practices, and ensure security measures are up to date

(b) **Upgrade/Grow:** As the user's needs evolve, they might upgrade to a higher tier of the platform or expand their usage by integrating additional features or modules.

Here are some common challenges, key lessons, and advice to keep in mind and benefit from at this stage:

DECODING PLATFORM PATTERNS

Challenges

- Difficulty in scaling up with growth
- Cost of upgrades and premium features
- Complexity in adding new functionalities
- Integration challenges with new tools or platforms
- Ensuring data consistency and integrity during upgrades
- Feedback loops and iterative improvements based on user

Major Learning

Scalability planning and resource allocation are essential

Recommendations

Plan upgrades carefully, test thoroughly before deployment, and communicate changes clearly to users

(c) **Replace or Retire:** Eventually, the platform may no longer meet the user's needs due to significant changes in their requirements or the platform's capabilities. The user may then decide to replace or retire the platform.

Here are some common challenges, key lessons, and advice to keep in mind and benefit from at this stage:

Challenges

- Data migration challenges
- Emotional or operational resistance to change
- Finding a suitable replacement with minimal disruption
- Ensuring continuity of service during transition
- Decommissioning old systems securely and safely
- Legal and compliance implications of data transfer

Major Learning

Strategic planning for end-of-life phases ensures smooth transitions

Recommendations

Have a detailed transition plan, including data migration and user training, to minimize disruption

In the retention phase, long-term success hinges on maintaining and upgrading the platform as necessary, while also planning for its eventual replacement or retirement. This stage is focused on sustaining the relationship, adapting to evolving needs, and ensuring that the platform continues to meet new requirements as they arise. Continuous improvement and strategic foresight are key to keeping the platform relevant and effective over time.

Where to Use the Platform Success Blueprint in the User's Journey

This table provides a clear and concise alignment of the user's journey with the essential components of the blueprint.

Platform User Journey Phase	Related Blueprint Face	Explanation
Introductory Phase	Core Business Domain	Aligns user needs with the platform's core offering. Ensures the platform's value proposition is clearly communicated.
Interest and Need Alignment	Platform Strategy & Business Models	Users evaluate the platform based on its unique value, pricing, and competitive positioning.
Onboarding	Platform Experience & Economization	Ensures a smooth, intuitive onboarding that showcases the platform's value, minimizing friction and ensuring initial user satisfaction.
Navigation Phase	Platform Technology Strategy & Ecosystem	Focuses on seamless integration into the user's daily routine, ensuring the platform works well with other tools and enhances overall user engagement.
Daily Usage	Platform experience & economisation Platform Design & Architecture	The design and architecture influence ease of use, stability, and the ability for users to integrate the platform into their workflows.
Retention Phase	Platform Development & Operations	Continuous improvement and high performance are key to retaining users, along with adding new features and maintaining platform relevance.
Community Building	Platform Ecosystem Growth	Fostering a vibrant community around the platform helps maintain long-term engagement and user loyalty.

Key Takeaways

- The platform user's journey progresses through three critical phases—Introduction, Navigation, and Retention. Each phase presents unique challenges and opportunities, requiring platforms to adapt, foster loyalty, and stay relevant.

- Users must be well-informed about these essentials to fully leverage key aspects, rather than encountering failures before realizing their importance.

- The Platform Success Blueprint aligns the user's journey with critical platform components, guiding users through a structured process that enhances their experience while ensuring adaptability and continuity.

- Retention is key to long-term success. Platforms must continuously innovate, upgrade features, and remain relevant to keep users engaged, while also planning for eventual transitions as user needs evolve.

Chapter Thirteen

Building Platforms: A Provider's Journey

"Platform providers' journeys shine through a strong foundation - strive to grow stronger and clearer with each step."

In the last two sections, we've thoroughly explored the essentials and success blueprints for technology-driven platforms, covering everything from strategic planning to the intricate details of platform design and development. We've also addressed challenges and solutions at each stage of the platform user's lifecycle in the previous chapter. This chapter shifts focus to platform providers, guiding readers in mapping their own experiences to the six-sided Platform Success Blueprint and identifying areas that may require more attention.

The journey of platform providers is distinct and complex. They encounter numerous opportunities but also face significant challenges, particularly in execution and scaling—both within their internal teams and across the broader ecosystem that includes consumers, users, and other stakeholders. In this chapter, we will explore these challenges and opportunities through complex case studies.

In Chapter 2, we examined the real challenges faced by platform companies, explored key factors driving the rapid growth of the platform space, and conducted a root cause analysis. Building on that foundation, and through the numerous examples shared in this book, it is evident that the platform provider's journey has evolved at a pace that often outstrips the industry's ability to scale and support these business models effectively. This chapter will delve deeper into these developments.

The scale and complexity of platform providers have grown dramatically. Initially, providers offered solutions that simplified specific functions or met user needs, all wrapped up in a platform. However, this space quickly expanded into more accessible, democratized models. At the same time, providers faced intense competition while discovering new markets full of potential. This mix of challenges and opportunities has driven platform providers to innovate and find new ways to scale and grow.

To illustrate this, let's consider a complex example from the IT industry: AWS (Amazon Web Services). AWS is a leader in public cloud services, offering a wide range of solutions that enable businesses to scale, innovate, and operate more efficiently in the cloud. AWS started with basic services like storage (S3) and computing

(EC2) before expanding into the XaaS (Anything as a Service) model, encompassing IaaS, PaaS, SaaS, and more. As AWS scaled globally and integrated numerous technologies, it evolved into a complex cloud services marketplace offering a vast array of services, platforms, and tools. Some of these represent high-level abstractions and managed services, while others are standalone options customers can choose from. However, not everything provided by AWS today qualifies as a platform (refer to the platform definition in Chapter 4 if needed).

This evolution reflects a broader trend across various industries—not just cloud providers—where companies in retail, e-commerce, automotive, pharmaceuticals, and beyond have transitioned from offering specific functionalities to embracing product- and service-based business models. This shift has placed significant demands on these companies to maintain their pace, requiring them to automate many repeatable and composable aspects of their journey while supporting ecosystem stability and ease through platform evolution.

The phenomenon described above is illustrated in the diagram below.

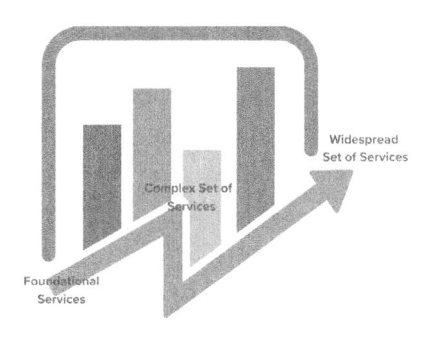

What's the Real Obstacle?

The primary challenge for platform providers is maintaining a cohesive platform experience while continuously expanding their services and products. Not all companies are as prepared or positioned for success as the public cloud leader, AWS, which manages to scale effectively. Without a focused strategy, platforms risk becoming fragmented, reducing the provider to a collection of unrelated services and products. This fragmentation can negatively impact both users and consumers, leading to a diluted platform experience.

For any platform provider, the key is to balance flexibility with standardization. Providers must scale, innovate, and expand while automating processes, enhancing user experience, fostering communities, and maintaining consistency.

To further visualize a platform provider's situation, imagine a large, intricately designed ship navigating the high seas, representing the platform provider's ecosystem. This ship is not just a vessel but a floating city, carrying numerous passengers who rely on its stability, comfort, and amenities. As the ship travels from one port to another, more passengers board, each with their unique needs and expectations. At the same time, new technologies, regulations, and trends demand constant upgrades and changes to the ship's infrastructure.

Now, consider the complexity involved: the ship's crew must keep the ship afloat, ensure smooth sailing, and prevent disruptions—all while adding new sections, upgrading old ones, and integrating cutting-edge technology to meet the evolving demands of the passengers. The ship must expand its facilities, upgrade safety measures, and enhance the passenger experience without compromising its stability or causing discomfort. At any moment, a miscalculation could lead to overloading or structural imbalance, endangering everyone on board.

This scenario mirrors the complexity of managing a platform, where the provider is tasked with innovating and integrating new features, maintaining existing infrastructure, and constantly iterating to enhance user experience. The provider must be vigilant in managing technical debt because a poorly designed platform can hinder its ability to adapt to ongoing changes. The challenges grow exponentially with the scale of the platform, making it crucial for the provider to balance growth with operational integrity, just as the ship's crew must balance expansion with the ship's stability.

At first glance, this analogy might seem like an exaggeration; however, it reflects the reality of today's IT industry and the immense complexity that platform companies face. This is why we now see shifts in dynamics happening more frequently, often every year, compared to earlier times when such changes occurred once a decade, or even less frequently, perhaps every two to three decades before. I hope this gives you a clearer understanding of the spiraling effect this has on the industry and the increasing challenges that platform providers must navigate.

The key point to focus on is the delicate balance platform providers must maintain between internal and external challenges as they scale and grow their businesses. Managing internal challenges is equally important, if not more so, because it significantly impacts the entire value chain. The balance between these internal and external challenges—and the attention each demands—is illustrated in the image above.

This is where platform engineering, internal developer platforms, open-source projects, and seamless integration play crucial roles, as emphasized throughout this book. These strategies help abstract dynamic components into service models and interfaces, which are essential in today's fast-evolving landscape. This also explains the growing emphasis on developer experience within the industry, enabling rapid development and changes. However, the industry must be cautious not to continually shift the burden of design and operations onto developers in the name of improving developer experience, as this is not a sustainable approach.

Sections B and C delve much deeper into these critical topics. This is why you need the Platform Success Blueprint more than ever to deal with the constant churn of platforms, providing a clearer and more systematic framework that this book has revealed.

This discussion leads us back to defining the platform provider's journey, which includes the following phases for success: Create, Assess, Change, gather Feedback, and Repeat. Unlike platform users, providers cannot simply opt out at any stage; their commitment is greater, and they face increasing complexity as they scale.

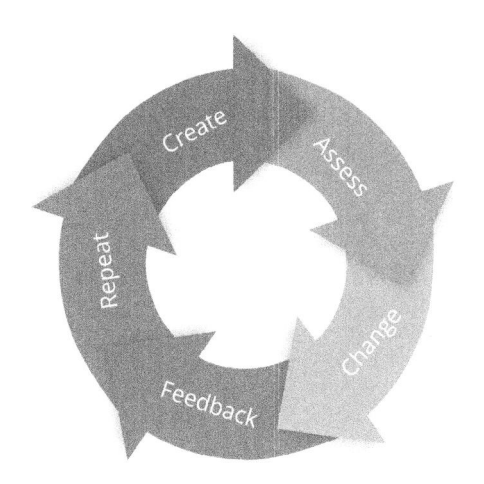

Let's break down each phase of the platform provider journey, outlining the challenges, key learnings, and actionable tips for success. This serves as a valuable resource for navigating the complexities of platform development and management.

Create (or Update) Phase

In the Create/Update phase, it's essential to establish a strong foundation that aligns with both your platform's vision and user needs. Prioritize a clear value proposition and build a scalable architecture from the start to ensure long-term success. Always keep the core business domain and platform strategy at the center of your efforts.

Here are some common challenges, key lessons, and advice to keep in mind and benefit from at this stage:

Challenges
- Defining a clear and unique value proposition
- Aligning platform features with user needs
- Securing initial funding and resources
- Building a scalable architecture from the start

Major Learning
- A clear vision and well-defined target audience are critical
- Initial platform design impacts long-term scalability and flexibility
- Early stakeholder buy-in can drive momentum

Recommendations
- Start with a Minimum Viable Product (MVP) to test and iterate quickly
- Focus on solving a specific problem for a defined user base
- Invest in a strong technical foundation that can scale

Assess Phase

In the assessment phase, the focus is on evaluating platform performance and identifying opportunities for improvement. Prioritize reviewing your technology strategy and design decisions at a pre-set frequency.

Here are some common challenges, key lessons, and advice to keep in mind and benefit from at this stage:

Challenges
- Gathering meaningful metrics and data
- Understanding user engagement and satisfaction
- Identifying gaps and areas for improvement
- Managing internal and external expectations

Major Learning
- Data-driven decisions lead to better outcomes
- Regular assessments help in staying aligned with market needs.
- Transparent communication with stakeholders builds trust

Recommendations
- Implement robust analytics tools to track key performance indicators (KPIs)
- Conduct regular platform users feedback sessions and surveys
- Stay agile and be ready to pivot based on assessment results

Change Phase

In the Change phase, careful management is essential to balance innovation with stability while minimizing disruption. Be mindful of any potential impact on technology or execution/ implementation.

Here are some common challenges, key lessons, and advice to keep in mind and benefit from at this stage:

Challenges

- Implementing changes without disrupting current users
- Balancing innovation with stability
- Overcoming resistance to change from internal teams
- Ensuring backward compatibility with previous versions

Major Learning

- Change is necessary for growth, but it must be managed carefully
- Continuous improvement requires a balance between new features and platform stability
- Effective change management strategies are crucial

Recommendations

- Plan and communicate changes clearly to all stakeholders
- Roll out changes incrementally to minimize disruption
- Ensure thorough testing and quality assurance before deploying changes

Feedback Phase

In the Feedback phase, gathering and integrating user insights is crucial for driving continuous platform improvement. Be sure to review the core business integration checklist (Chapter 6) from time to time and gather internal stakeholders feedback as well.

Here are some common challenges, key lessons, and advice to keep in mind and benefit from at this stage:

Challenges

- Collecting and analyzing feedback effectively
- Distinguishing between valuable feedback and noise
- Addressing negative feedback constructively
- Integrating feedback into the development cycle

Major Learning

- Continuous feedback loops drive platform improvement
- Constructive feedback helps in refining the platform's offerings
- Engaging with users builds a loyal community

Recommendations

- Establish multiple channels for feedback collection (e.g., surveys, forums, direct communication)
- Prioritize feedback based on impact and feasibility
- Use feedback to guide the product roadmap and future development

Repeat Phase

In the Repeat phase, the goal is to sustain momentum and drive continuous innovation through successive iterations.

Here are some common challenges, key lessons, and advice to keep in mind and benefit from at this stage:

Challenges
- Maintaining momentum over multiple iterations
- Avoiding stagnation or complacency
- Ensuring continuous innovation
- Managing the cumulative complexity of multiple iterations

Major Learning
- Iteration is key to staying competitive and relevant
- The success of previous phases informs future cycles
- Continuous iteration can lead to significant long-term gains

Recommendations
- Treat each cycle as an opportunity for growth and improvement
- Keep the core mission in focus while iterating
- Regularly revisit and refine the platform blueprint based on lessons learned

Guidance on Blueprint Usage

This blueprint serves as a guiding framework throughout the platform-building process and lifecycle. It should be thoroughly understood by you, your team, and your organization to ensure a shared understanding among everyone involved in building the platform. This shared understanding will maximize the blueprint's practical application and unlock the immense value it will deliver in the coming years.

Last but not least: Innovation, security, and measurement (metrics review) are integral to every phase of the platform journey. These elements are depicted in the image below as part of a continuous process.

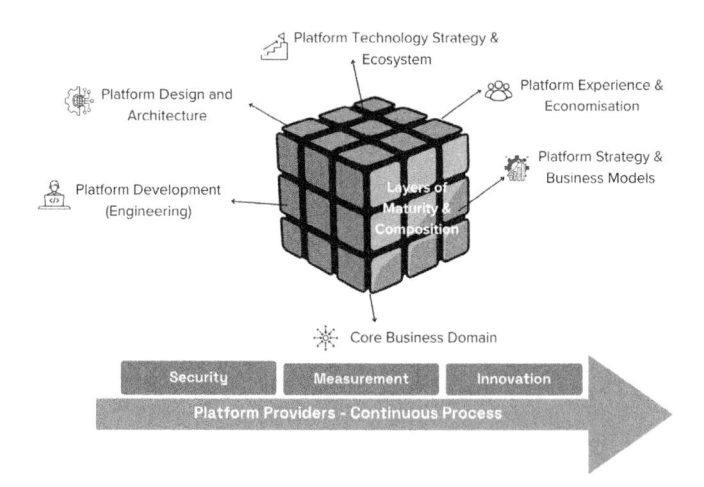

Platform Technology Strategy & Ecosystem

Platform Design and Architecture

Platform Experience & Economisation

Platform Development (Engineering)

Platform Strategy & Business Models

Layers of Maturity & Composition

Core Business Domain

Security | Measurement | Innovation
Platform Providers - Continuous Process

Summarizing the provider's journey, this chapter provided a comprehensive overview of the platform provider journey, highlighting the critical phases, obstacles, and actionable insights necessary for success. By breaking down each phase, from initial development to ongoing management, we explored the intricacies of platform building, offering practical guidance to navigate the complexities that arise. The chapter emphasized the importance of a well-defined blueprint as a guiding framework, ensuring that all team members and stakeholders share a common understanding of the platform's goals and processes. Innovation, security, and metrics review were underscored as continuous, integral components throughout the platform lifecycle, reinforcing the need for a holistic approach to platform development.

In the next chapter, we will explore Apple's platform patterns as a case study. By examining the company's strategies, decisions, and challenges, we aim to provide valuable insights into how one of the world's most successful companies navigated its platform journey to achieve industry dominance. This case study will serve as a powerful example of how the principles and strategies discussed in this book can be applied in real-world scenarios. Let's zoom out!

Key Takeaways

- Mastering the phases of Create, Assess, Change, Feedback, and Repeat is crucial for successful platform management.

- Providers must balance flexibility with standardization to maintain a cohesive platform experience while scaling.

- A well-understood platform blueprint ensures a shared vision and strategy among all team members.

- Emphasizing platform engineering and developer experience is key to managing complexity and driving innovation.

- Continuous adaptation and innovation are essential to staying competitive in the platform provider space.

Chapter Fourteen

Case Study - Apple's Platform Patterns

"Apple's platform journey is a masterclass; harness it from the lens of the Platform Success Blueprint."

Apple Inc., a multinational technology giant, is synonymous with innovation in hardware, software, and scalable platforms. Over the past few decades, the company has become a household name, with products like the iPhone, iPad, Mac, Apple Watch, and Apple TV becoming integral parts of modern life. However, its success is not merely a result of its innovations—it stems from decades of strategic planning, meticulous execution, and an evolving platform strategy.

In 2021, the company sold about 24% of the 1.43 billion smartphones purchased globally, underscoring the massive scale at which the company operates[1]. It continued to dominate the top-10 best-selling smartphones list in Q2 2024, showcasing its sustained market leadership[2].

This might prompt a common question: Is this technology giant primarily a product company or a platform company? The answer lies in its unique approach, where its product and platform strategies are seamlessly integrated. Unlike companies such as Google or Meta, which started purely as platform businesses, Apple's strategy offers valuable insights into combining hardware and platforms—a synergy this case study will explore through the lens of the Platform Success Blueprint. If you haven't read the foundation sections mentioned in the Introduction, it is highly encouraged that you do so at this point to fully absorb and understand this case study.

Apple identifies itself as a 'Technology company,' where platforms play an integral role in its core business model, benefiting users, consumers, and partners alike. The company offers a range of hardware products, all powered by a highly customized operating system, a suite of core in-house software, and various other platforms that amplify its network effects globally.

Company's modern platform journey can be traced back to Steve Jobs' iconic vision encapsulated in the phrase, '*1,000 songs in your pocket*' referring to the first iPod. From that pivotal moment, the company has continuously innovated, expanding its offerings to include mature products, platforms, frameworks, and tools that serve millions worldwide.

The tech giant's technology strategy is intricately tied to its premium hardware offerings. Despite the challenges and occasional setbacks in scaling their platforms, the company consistently demonstrates resilience and adaptability, providing valuable lessons for other platform providers.

Between 1997 and 2017, the tech giant grew 300 times in value[3], a testament to its relentless innovation in design, technology maturity, and strategic leadership. Managing this exponential growth would have been impossible without leveraging digital platforms, globalization, open standards, and a robust business model—pillars we explored in Chapter 2. This journey exemplifies how a platform-driven approach can catalyze growth and innovation, making it a powerful and relevant case study for understanding the practical application of the Platform Success Blueprint.

Let's dive deeper into how this strategy aligns with the broader landscape of technology and product offerings, and what valuable lessons we can learn from its journey.

Platform – Network Effects and Offerings

Apple is renowned for crafting products that cater to its end users, but its equal strength lies in its ability to create platforms that serve a broader audience—partners, integrators, internal developers, and, in some cases, the end users themselves. This strategic approach allows the company to seamlessly integrate its hardware with the evolving technological landscape through robust platforms. These platforms are customized to meet the diverse needs of its various stakeholders, as illustrated in the diagram below:

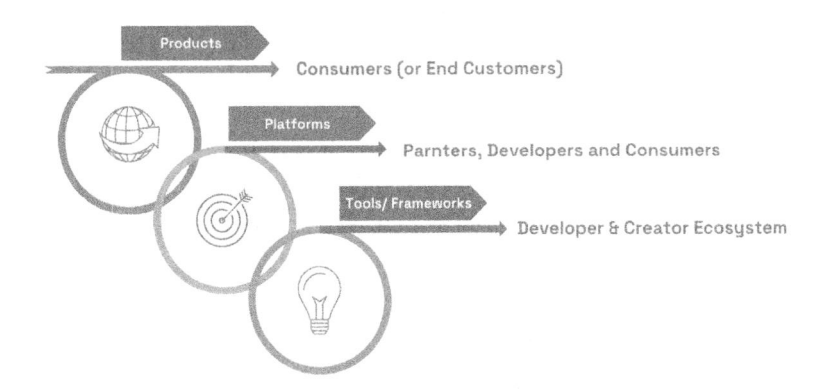

```
Products
  ──────────▶ Consumers (or End Customers)
     Platforms
       ──────────▶ Parnters, Developers and Consumers
         Tools/ Frameworks
           ──────────▶ Developer & Creator Ecosystem
```

Its ecosystem is a complex web of technology-driven entities, including Products (Core Business Domain), Platforms (Foundation), Programming Frameworks (Developer Ecosystem), and a range of tools, technologies, and platforms from various vendors. These components collaborate to form a cohesive and innovative environment, positioning the company as a leader in the tech industry.

But there's more to the story—let's delve deeper by connecting Apple's approach to the Platform, identifying the strategies behind its remarkable success. Steve Jobs famously said, 'Good artists copy, great artists steal,' emphasizing the importance of learning from existing ideas and refining them. In the same way, I encourage you to absorb the lessons from this book and apply them to this case study, making the insights your own.

Its platforms can be broadly categorized into two groups, each playing a pivotal role in the company's success:

1. **Core Business Platforms** - These platforms are integral to company's products and enable partners to build or integrate strong foundational elements. Key examples include the operating systems iOS and macOS, the online storage and device management platform iCloud, and the application ecosystem platform, the App Store.

2. **Internal/External Platforms** - These platforms are either used internally to support various operational aspects or offered to partners for integration. Examples include Apple Business Manager, Apple School Manager, and AppleCare for Enterprise.

As we explore these platforms, we'll uncover key patterns and strategies that have been instrumental in in the company's success.

Apple's Platform: Leveraging the Platform Success Blueprint

This image on next page should help reflect on the technological entities within companies. From here, we will explore all six sides of the Platform Success Blueprint to relate it to everything we've learned so far.

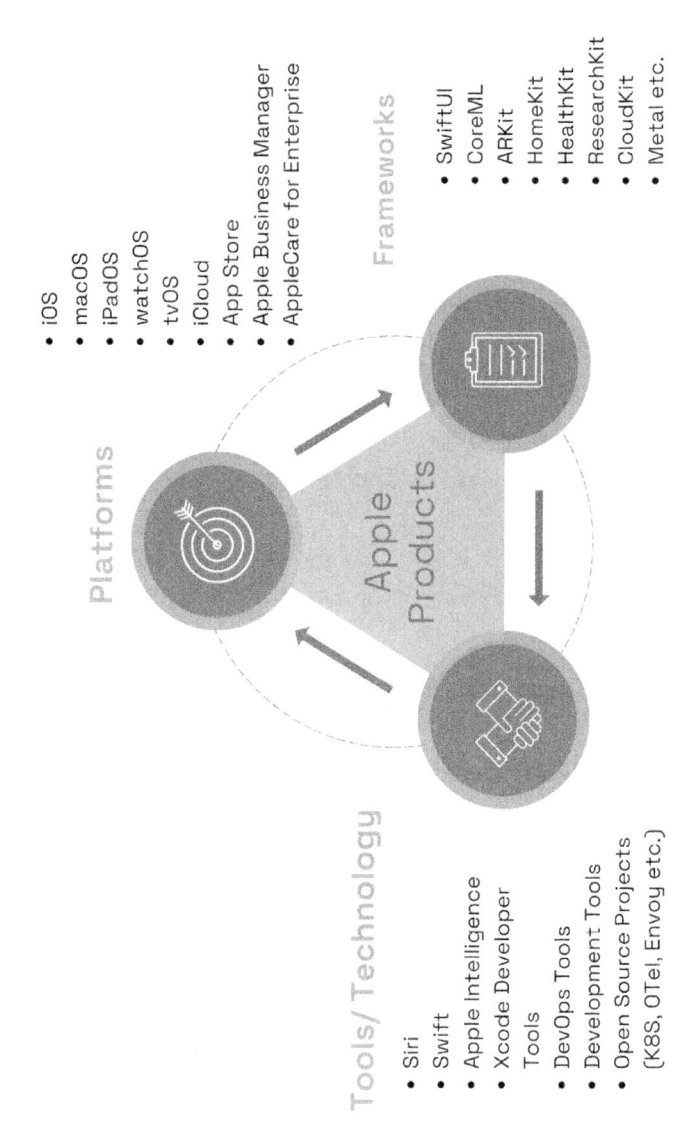

Platforms
- iOS
- macOS
- iPadOS
- watchOS
- tvOS
- iCloud
- App Store
- Apple Business Manager
- AppleCare for Enterprise

Frameworks
- SwiftUI
- CoreML
- ARKit
- HomeKit
- HealthKit
- ResearchKit
- CloudKit
- Metal etc.

Tools/Technology
- Siri
- Swift
- Apple Intelligence
- Xcode Developer Tools
- DevOps Tools
- Development Tools
- Open Source Projects (K8S, OTel, Envoy etc.)

Apple Products

Core Business Domain

Every decision and strategy at Apple is deeply rooted in its core business needs, as reflected in the evolution of its platforms and strategic decisions that set the company apart. If you've ever used one of its devices, you'll recognize the unparalleled security, stability, and sustainability that its products and platforms offer.

Sustainability is embedded in the company's operations and serves as a key component of its platform strategy. The company has taken this commitment to the next level by pledging to achieve net-zero carbon emissions across its entire footprint by 2030[4]. This ambitious goal integrates seamlessly with their value chain, requiring platforms and technologies to support these sustainability efforts. For example, the iPhone trade-in program demonstrates how it incorporates sustainability into its platform ecosystem by refurbishing, reselling, or recycling old devices, thereby supporting a circular economy.

The company is often referred to as a "walled garden" due to its controlled environment, which contrasts with more open systems like Android or Linux. However, this balance between control and openness is one of its strengths, providing users with a secure and trusted experience. This strategy has been pivotal in differentiating the company from its competitors. This also reminds us about the platform approach (open, closed, or middle ground) we explored earlier.

The organizational structure deviates from traditional business functions[5] —a shift Steve Jobs implemented after becoming CEO. Rather than aligning with conventional business units, the company emphasizes owning decisions, focusing on design, and sustaining those decisions through work products. The company's leadership is characterized by three key traits: deep expertise, immersion in details, and a willingness to collaborate through debate. This approach has fostered coordinated decision-making and a cohesive platform strategy as well.

A key aspect of its platform strategy is its rigorous design and integration process. Even today, the final design approval for products and changes must go through an executive review—a practice initiated early on. This ensures that every product aligns with the company's brand values and meets the company's high standards for quality and innovation. Once a design is approved, detailed specifications are created for manufacturing and integration with platforms like the App Store and iCloud, highlighting the importance of alignment between product design and platform capabilities.

Effective platform integration within a business context requires clear guidance. The company's approach underscores the importance of aligning platform capabilities with business objectives, ensuring seamless integration that contributes meaningfully to overall business success.

The core business domain and expertise have always been at the center of everything Apple does.

Platform Strategy & Business Model

Platform strategy is central to managing the massive scale at which it operates today, offering valuable lessons for companies navigating platform-driven business models. The company has developed some of the most scalable products and platforms globally, showcasing a robust and highly integrated ecosystem. A prime example is its in-house operating system, which serves as the backbone for all its products. While core functions remain consistent across devices, the system is customized for each platform—whether iOS, macOS, tvOS, or the newer visionOS. This critical differentiation has never been outsourced; instead, the operating system has been optimized internally to ensure security, technological leverage, and adaptability across devices.

The following illustration helps visualize the differentiation of its technology offerings and provides a sneak peek into the company's innovations.

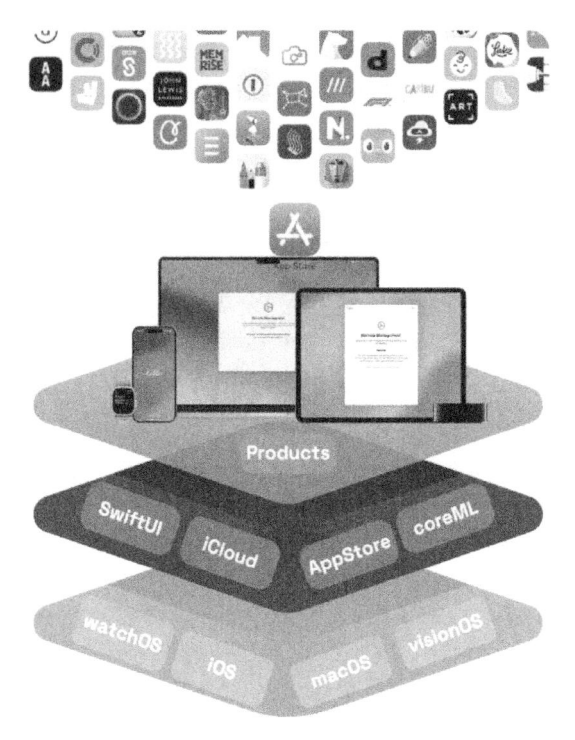

These systems are designed with flexible tools and frameworks that offer both stability and innovation. The combination of the operating system with programming frameworks like SwiftUI and HomeKit provides developers and users with freedom and flexibility. This ecosystem supports a vast array of applications and ensures a seamless user experience across all Apple devices.

The introduction of iCloud in 2011 was a significant milestone in Apple's platform strategy and enhancement. iCloud provided cloud storage and synchronization services across all Apple devices, further enhancing the interconnectedness of its ecosystem and seamless user experience. By 2021, iCloud had over 850 million users, deeply integrating into the daily lives of Apple's customers and reinforcing the company's platform-centric approach.

iCloud itself, while offered as a service to customers, represents a remarkable integration of multiple platforms.

Apple's focus on security and customer privacy is implemented through various platform-layer security features, including the Secure Enclave—a dedicated secure subsystem integrated into Apple devices[6] that manages cryptographic operations, protects user data, and stores sensitive information such as biometric data.

This tech giant dominates the personal technology space. Initially, ideas like a soft keyboard and practical calligraphy faced scepticism. However, what was once seen as disruptive innovation has now positioned the company as a leader, even challenging Microsoft and other players in the personal computing space. Its platform strategy has also enabled organizations to manage their device deployment projects, integrating hardware, software, apps, and services while providing control and flexibility on a large scale.

Apple's platform business model supports a wide range of interactions, including:

- **B2B**: Apple collaborates with companies like IBM and Deloitte to deliver custom enterprise solutions using Apple devices and software. Businesses also rely on Apple's Mobile Device Management (MDM) and fleet management solutions to manage and secure their fleets of iPhones, iPads, and Macs.

- **B2C**: Apple operates retail stores worldwide and the App Store, offering a direct point of purchase for apps, music, movies, and more.

- **B2D**: Apple provides developers with essential tools like Xcode and Swift, along with the App Store platform, enabling them to distribute apps to millions of users.

- **C2C**: Platforms like the App Store facilitate a consumer-to-consumer model, where individual developers can sell their apps. Apple Pay supports peer-to-peer payments in this model.

- **B2G**: Apple offers tailored solutions for educational institutions and government agencies, enhancing operational efficiency and ensuring compliance.

Next, let's explore one of the most sophisticated yet straightforward principles behind this pioneering company's products: the emphasis on user experience and refinement. As Jony Ive, Apple's former Chief Design Officer, famously said, *'It's very easy to be different, but very difficult to be better.'*[7] This quote reflects Apple's design philosophy of striving for excellence over mere novelty. Ive's influence has been integral to the company's success, where innovation means not just standing out, but genuinely enhancing the user experience.

Platform experience and economization

Apple's user experience is widely regarded as unmatched, known for its sleek, minimalist design combined with a strong commitment to user privacy and security. These elements go beyond aesthetics—they reflect the value system established, maintained, and upheld by the company's leadership. The "Think Different" ethos continues to drive customer loyalty to Apple stores and products.

Excelling at streamlining its service blueprint, Apple optimizes the user experience to ensure that every interaction with its products is intuitive and satisfying.

The company has continuously evolved, learning from both successes and setbacks. Not all innovations have hit the mark. For example, Apple Pay, while a well-conceived idea, initially faced challenges. After its launch in September 2014, the service struggled to gain traction, suggesting it didn't offer enough value to replace the convenience of traditional credit cards.[8] However, over time, as more retailers adopted the service and consumers became more familiar with it, Apple Pay slowly gained momentum and has now become an integral part of users' lives, offering a seamless experience in many countries.

One of Apple's strengths has evolved into allowing customers to create their own experiences. Despite its history of tightly controlling information, the company recognized the need for flexibility and customization. The creation of the App Store enabled external developers and creators to modify and enhance the product experience, leading to a richer and more personalized user experience. With hundreds of thousands of apps available, Apple takes a cut of the sales while customers enjoy a highly customized experience on their iPhone and iPad platforms, emulating network effects and ensuring consistency at every step.

Apple's recent announcement in Q3 2024 about iOS 18's new payment feature, 'Tap to Cash', exemplifies this ongoing innovation[9]. This feature significantly enhances the peer-to-peer payment experience, demonstrating the company's ability to adapt and refine its offerings to meet user needs.

These examples highlight that while brand's focus on user experience is a key strength, even the most well-designed products must address real user needs, habits and evolving trends to achieve widespread adoption.

Platform Technology Strategy and Ecosystem

The tech giant's ability to fully integrate its vision into technology is remarkable. The company excels in design and systems thinking, with a strong emphasis on ecosystem integration. Security is a fundamental part of the Apple experience, deeply embedded in every aspect of their products.

Apple's Worldwide Developers Conference (WWDC) is a pivotal event where the company showcases its latest technologies and platforms to developers worldwide. Open source plays a crucial role in Apple's ecosystem, with Swift being a prime example. Introduced at WWDC 2014, Swift was initially proprietary but became open-source in 2015 under the Apache License 2.0, allowing developers on Apple's platforms and Linux to utilize it freely. By 2018, Swift was ranked among the top ten programming languages and was the number one choice for developing iOS mobile apps, according to the TIOBE Index.[10]

Apple strategically maintains a relatively closed ecosystem compared to competitors, fostering deep user engagement and loyalty. This approach makes it challenging for users to switch to other platforms. Nevertheless, company engages sufficiently with the broader tech community, as evidenced by its membership in the

CNCF[11] as a Platinum End User Member and its collaborative efforts with companies like Google, IBM, AWS, Azure and more.

The company's technology strategy focuses on developing opinionated Kubernetes tooling to address hybrid cloud challenges and manage Kubernetes clusters for scalability and performance. By leveraging CNCF projects like Kubernetes, gRPC, Prometheus, Envoy Proxy, and Vitess, the company ensures seamless infrastructure management across private and public clouds. Security remains a top priority, incorporating comprehensive Role-Based Access Control (RBAC) to manage user permissions effectively. Modern practices like GitOps, CI/CD pipelines, and Infrastructure as Code (IaC) further streamline development. Comprehensive monitoring and secure traffic management, powered by Prometheus and Envoy Proxy, reinforce its robust cloud strategy. Though Apple rarely discusses it openly, these technologies and their effective usage are indispensable for a company of this scale.

All of these technologies, along with the broader tech landscape, contribute to Apple's network effects. For instance, in 2022, App Store developers generated $1.1 trillion in total billings and sales within the App Store ecosystem, underscoring Apple's commitment to fostering a strong developer community and maximizing the potential of its App Store platform[12].

To address expertise gaps in these complex environments, Apple invests significantly in training and hiring skilled professionals and strongly supports the open-source ecosystem, such as its contributions to CNCF projects. However, like many technology-centric companies, Apple faces the industry-wide challenge of a shortage of skilled resources, which is reflected in both its hiring patterns and the roles within its platform teams. Despite these challenges, Apple continues to push the boundaries of what is possible with technology, maintaining its position as a leader in the industry.

Platform Design and Architecture

Apple's philosophy is deeply embedded in a design and architectural mindset that has been nurtured and refined over time. What we see from Apple today is the result of these foundational principles.

For a deeper understanding of how this culture has been cultivated within the ecosystem, and the contributions of numerous unsung heroes who brought this vision to life, I recommend reading *Creative Selection* by Ken Kocienda. This book highlights key experiences and how the company nurtured its design and architectural decisions through multiple iterations before finalizing the design.

When it comes to integrating software, such as operating systems and user interfaces, Apple's software team is pivotal in ensuring that hardware and software work in perfect harmony. The development of operating systems like iOS, macOS, and watchOS is closely synchronized with the hardware design process. This level of integration results in a seamless user experience, where the software feels finely tuned to the hardware. For example, the introduction of Face ID in the iPhone required significant collaboration between software developers and hardware engineers to ensure it functioned reliably and securely.

Apple's R&D and prototyping teams work hand-in-hand with engineering teams to create prototypes. This phase includes developing new technologies, rigorous testing, and refining product features. This collaborative and iterative process is central to com-

DECODING PLATFORM PATTERNS

pany's ability to innovate and maintain its leadership in the tech industry.

The evolution of platform architecture is a co-creational effort, requiring collaboration between the platform provider, orchestrators, and complementors (as shown in diagram below). In the Apple ecosystem, for instance, the iPhone serves as the core platform (platform provider), the App Store acts as the orchestrator, managing and coordinating app distribution and quality, and third-party app developers are the complementors, adding value by creating applications that enhance the user experience. Understanding these roles and the need for continuous evolution is crucial for maintaining a robust, innovative platform that aligns with a long-term vision.

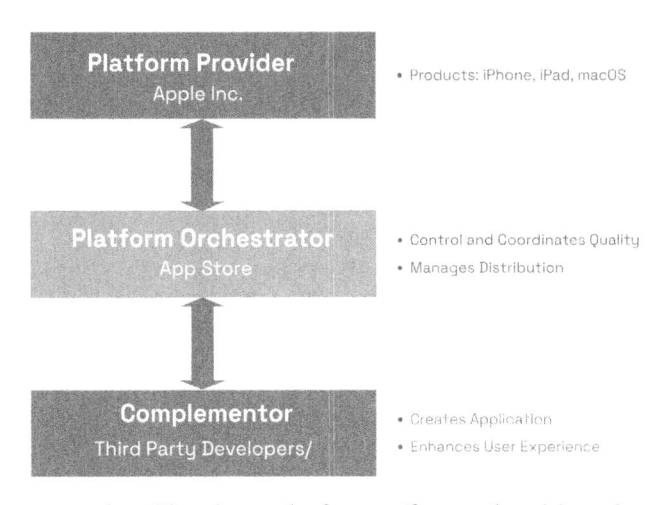

Platform Provider
Apple Inc.
- Products: iPhone, iPad, macOS

Platform Orchestrator
App Store
- Control and Coordinates Quality
- Manages Distribution

Complementor
Third Party Developers/
- Creates Application
- Enhances User Experience

Another example, iCloud is a platform offering cloud-based storage services and app servers for end customers, designed to store data such as documents, photos, music, device backups, and app data. iCloud is an essential part of the ecosystem, ensuring customers do not lose data, files, or device setups even if an Apple product is lost, stolen, or damaged. It also includes a set of cloud-based web apps. The iCloud platform scales to support hundreds of millions of users worldwide, demonstrating Apple's ability to maintain performance and reliability on an extraordinary scale. It embodies critical non-functional requirements (NFRs) such as scalability, security, and reliability—key aspects discussed in detail as essential platform architecture principles in Chapter 10.

These elements underscore the company's integrated design and practices, which form the foundation of its products, building a powerful, interoperable, and interconnected ecosystem that supports a wide range of interactions while fostering both innovation and user loyalty.

Platform Development

Platform development is a remarkable case of collaboration, confidentiality, rigorous testing, and a relentless focus on experience, integration and quality. This methodology has been key to the company's success in consistently delivering innovative, high-performing products.

Apple's development journey began not only with the creation of groundbreaking hardware and software but also with the establishment of an innovative approach to work. The company prioritized flexibility over rigid methodologies, recognizing that adaptability is crucial in platform development[13]. As some senior officials have noted, there was no fixed checklist for how things were done at Apple; instead, processes evolved, adapting to the needs of each project and the demands of the market.

At the heart of Apple's development process is interdisciplinary collaboration. Cross-functional teams—comprising platform engineers, designers, and product managers from various departments—work closely on each project.

Apple's vertical integration strategy plays a crucial role in this process. By controlling as much of the product lifecycle as possible—from designing custom chips like the A-series processors to developing proprietary software—Apple optimizes the interaction between hardware and software. This deep integration allows the company to create products that are not only powerful but also seamless in their operation.

Confidentiality is another hallmark of Apple's development approach. Even within the company, teams often work on projects without knowing the full scope, and information is shared on a need-to-know basis. This culture of confidentiality helps prevent leaks and preserves the element of surprise for product launches. Security measures are strictly enforced, with secure development environments, encrypted communications, and rigorous background checks for employees working on sensitive projects.

To ensure the highest quality, Apple conducts rigorous testing throughout the development process. Employees often engage in "dogfooding," where they use unreleased products internally to identify issues and refine the user experience. This internal testing phase is crucial for catching bugs and ensuring that the product is ready for public release.

Apple leverages advanced development tools like Xcode, along with custom internal platforms for continuous integration (CI), bug tracking, and project management. These tools support the entire development lifecycle, from code integration to deployment. Additionally, proprietary internal platforms manage automated testing, code integration, and deployment processes, further enhancing the efficiency and reliability of its development efforts. Much of this internal infrastructure has never been publicly shared.

A feedback loop is integral to Apple's development strategy. The company continuously gathers feedback from its products in the market, which informs updates, improvements, and the development of new products. This ongoing cycle of feedback and refinement ensures that Apple's platforms and products evolve in response to user needs and market trends.

Overall, Apple's platform development approach is a carefully orchestrated process that blends an innovative work culture, strong collaboration, vertical (or more) integrations, confidentiality, rigorous testing, and continuous improvement. Like other major technology companies, it faces its share of challenges. However, by focusing not only on products but also on fostering a flexible and evolving approach to innovation through platforms, the company has maintained its leadership in the industry, consistently delivering products that exceed user expectations.

Platform Journey

Apple's platform journey, much like that of any leading provider, begins with the creation phase and progresses through an iterative development process that continually evolves. Each iteration refines the platform, integrating lessons learned and introducing innovations. The success of the change phase, where the platform adapts to meet new demands, depends on the quality of decisions made in earlier phases. Strong decisions enable seamless transitions and sustained growth, while poor choices may require significant adjustments to keep the platform on course.

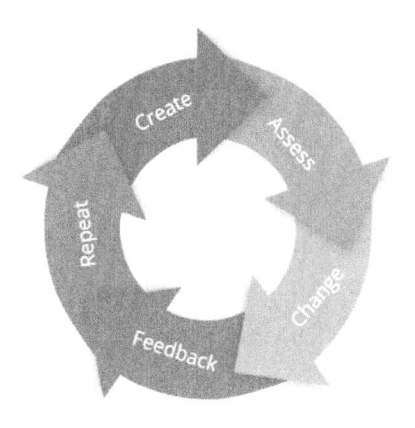

All of this, while navigating constantly evolving platforms that serve millions (like the ship analogy discussed in detail earlier in Chapter 13). As you can see, not everything technology offers qualifies as a platform. A true platform, however, fulfills its purpose by providing stability to its users alongside clear integrations, all while operating in a constantly evolving environment serving millions.

In summary, Apple's platform journey exemplifies the critical elements of successful platform development, as outlined in the Platform Success Blueprint. By starting with a strong foundation rooted in core business needs, the company has built a cohesive and integrated ecosystem that continues to innovate and grow. The iterative nature of its development process ensures that each phase builds on the previous one, allowing for seamless transitions and sustained progress. This ongoing refinement, coupled with strategic alignment and a relentless focus on user experience, underscores why it remains a leader in the technology industry.

I believe that says it all! We've covered an incredible amount of detail in this case study, touching on a wide range of insights. This resource is a goldmine of knowledge[14], offering valuable lessons well worth your time to thoroughly understand and absorb. I highly recommend revisiting it periodically to reinforce these insights and continue learning from them.

---

1. https://seaopenresearch.eu/Journals/articles/NIS_21_7.pdf

DECODING PLATFORM PATTERNS

2. https://www.counterpointresearch.com/insights/global-top-10-best-selling-smartphones-q2-2024/

3. https://hbr.org/2020/11/how-apple-is-organized-for-innovation

4. https://www.apple.com/uk/environment/

5. https://hbr.org/2020/11/how-apple-is-organized-for-innovation

6. https://support.apple.com/en-gb/guide/security/sec59b0b31ff/web

7. https://www.amazon.com/Jony-Ive-Genius-Greatest-Products/dp/B09TCQ3SY3/ref=sr_1_1?crid=WWBIX3F2TKQY&dib=eyJ2IjoiMSJ9.nmlmvor8xw98ZabiUsKKgA._N_RHmGz3n1EfH6ldZfM47Q0koowVlEEeiu8V6NVM8Y&dib_tag=se&keywords=The+Telegraph+and+the+book+Jony+Ive%3A+The+Genius+Behind+Apple%27s&qid=1725573113&sprefix=the+telegraph+and+the+book+jony+ive+the+genius+behind+apple%27s%2Caps%2C192&sr=8-1

8. https://www.globenewswire.com/news-release/2015/10/27/780466/37330/en/Phoenix-Marketing-International-Releases-New-Data-Revealing-the-Ongoing-Challenges-Surrounding-Apple-Pay.html

9. https://www.apple.com/newsroom/2024/06/new-features-come-to-apple-services-this-fall/

10. https://meterpreter.org/tiobe-october-2018/?utm_content=cmp-true

11. https://www.cncf.io/blog/2019/06/11/apple-joins-cloud-native-computing-foundation-as-platinum-end-user-member/

12. https://www.apple.com/newsroom/2023/05/developers-generated-one-point-one-trillion-in-the-app-store-ecosystem-in-2022/

13. https://www.amazon.com/Creative-Selection-Ken-Kocienda-audiobook/dp/B07FG81B7W/ref=sr_1_1?crid=2X8FCCPGKU7LM&dib=eyJ2IjoiMSJ9.Trqj4733FCtfV92zR7arHJaipJ5p5q2tM5HK7lJwn0s.y9vN39crMy7bLAq-kb11wCEMeE10ZrEqQhZ1sRWHBAs&dib_tag=se&keywords=Creative+Selection+by+Ken+Kocienda&qid=1725576864&sprefix=creative+selection+by+ken+kocienda%2Caps%2C213&sr=8-1

14. Disclaimer: The data and insights presented in this case study are based solely on publicly available information, including a comprehensive review of existing literature on Apple's technologies, developer ecosystem, design principles, platform strategies, target audience, competitive landscape, and market trends. Additionally, information has been sourced from books and reputable online sources that are freely accessible to the public. No confidential or proprietary information has been used. All material discussed is widely known or available in the public domain, and any conclusions drawn are entirely my own based on this research.

Chapter Fifteen

Future of Platforms with AI/ ML

"The future of platforms will favour not those who move the fastest, but those who build trust, fairness, and deliver exceptional experiences."

The landscape of digital platforms is on the brink of a profound transformation, fueled by rapid advancements in Artificial Intelligence (AI) and Machine Learning (ML). These technologies are set to redefine how organizations build, deploy, and evolve their technological ecosystems. In this chapter, we will explore the emerging trends that are shaping the future of platforms and analyze their potential impacts, along with the preparedness required to navigate these changes.

Late 2022 marked a significant turning point as we entered the era of Generative AI disruption, ushering in a wave of AI-driven innovation. This new phase has introduced advanced platform features and integrations that are evolving at an unprecedented pace. With the advent of generative AI, platforms now possess capabilities such as easily summarizing complex and large-scale content, automating intricate processes, and enhancing user interactions with remarkable sophistication. These advancements necessitate a re-evaluation and adaptation of existing platform strategies to fully leverage the potential of applied AI and ML across various applications and industries.

As we prepare for this next wave of technological advancement, several critical questions arise:

- How will AI/ML impact existing platforms?

- Will traditional technology platforms undergo significant transformations?

- What new forms of churn might emerge in platform usage and development?

- What are the potential risks and opportunities associated with these changes?

- How can organizations remain competitive and adaptable in this evolving landscape?

This chapter aims to address these crucial questions by exploring effective strategies for understanding and harnessing AI/ML platform patterns smartly and efficiently.

Drawing from my experience working with diverse platforms and technologies, I predict that numerous new-age platform patterns will continue to emerge. We are already witnessing the integration of small, intelligent features into everyday tools and platforms—evident in personalized recommendations on services like YouTube, Amazon, and Instagram, as well as in auto-suggestion functionalities in content creation and image generation tools. One particularly advanced feature is real-time personalized content generation, where platforms like Amazon and Netflix dynamically create and deliver content tailored to individual users based on their behavior and interactions. This goes beyond earlier recommendation systems by enabling platforms to generate personalized product descriptions, dynamic playlists, and content summaries that adapt in real time. These integrations are reshaping user experiences by providing more tailored and efficient interactions, making platforms more responsive and engaging than ever before.

Platforms have been disrupted in the past and will continue to be in the future. We are moving toward a future where we will own fewer physical products like cars, bikes, vacation homes, household tools, web hosting services, IT infrastructure, and storage solutions. Instead, we will increasingly contract for more services directly with one another, likely managed through peer-to-peer transaction platforms supported by versatile digital technologies like blockchain to enable more secure and transparent exchanges.

The most important and welcome news is that the core principles and the 'Platform success Blueprint' will remain unchanged, even as innovations add layers of granularity and complexity. However, if you stick to these principles and keep the foundation aligned, this new-age granularity will be manageable. These foundational concepts may be supplemented by additional cubelets (areas of work) to accommodate the growing intricacies of the technological landscape.

This shift underscores the importance of building platforms grounded in trust and fairness, providing seamless and enriching experiences that adapt to users' evolving needs. As AI and ML continue to advance, organizations that embrace these principles will be best positioned to thrive in the dynamic future of digital platforms.

Anticipating the Next Wave: Predicting the Future of Technology Platforms

Before diving deep into future platform patterns, let's take a moment to predict how the next decade might unfold. It wouldn't surprise me if these advancements happen sooner than anticipated, making the 2030s a decade of transformative platforms and features. We must build with rapid changes in mind and be prepared to adapt to the ever-evolving technological landscape.

Decades of Innovation
2030s

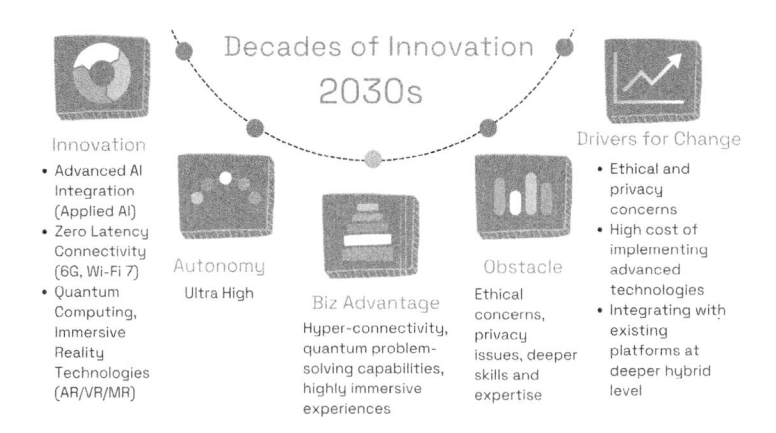

Innovation
- Advanced AI Integration (Applied AI)
- Zero Latency Connectivity (6G, Wi-Fi 7)
- Quantum Computing, Immersive Reality Technologies (AR/VR/MR)

Autonomy
Ultra High

Biz Advantage
Hyper-connectivity, quantum problem-solving capabilities, highly immersive experiences

Obstacle
Ethical concerns, privacy issues, deeper skills and expertise

Drivers for Change
- Ethical and privacy concerns
- High cost of implementing advanced technologies
- Integrating with existing platforms at deeper hybrid level

Today, quantum technology is at a stage comparable to conventional computing in the early 1960s—centralized and accessible only to a few companies that can afford to research and experiment with it. IBM and Google, among others, are leading the charge. Quantum computers are challenging and costly to construct and program, predominantly found in universities and corporate research labs. Despite this, quantum computing remains groundbreaking, with the potential to drive new types of specialized applications such as simulation, optimization, cryptography, and secure communication[1].

Challenges and Opportunities for Future Platforms

The future evolution of digital platforms will be shaped by emerging technologies and evolving user expectations. Next-generation platforms are set to deliver more immersive and personalized experiences through innovations like augmented reality, virtual reality, and AI-driven personalization, opening up new opportunities for businesses to meet individual needs. However, these advancements bring challenges, particularly around managing granularity, regulatory scrutiny, ethical concerns, and data privacy. Staying ahead of these issues will be essential for maintaining trust. Technologies like quantum computing and advanced AI will also pose new challenges and opportunities, requiring robust planning and adaptation in platform development.

The Role of Data Fabrics in AI-Driven Architectures

Data fabrics, which provide a unified architecture for managing data across platforms, will play a crucial role in future AI-driven architectures. As AI workflows become more integrated into these platforms, data fabrics will need to evolve to support real-time data access and processing with greater flexibility. This evolution presents an opportunity for platforms to enhance their data integration capabilities, enabling more robust AI-driven insights and faster decision-making. Emphasizing data engineering, governance, and democratization will be key to allowing legitimate access to data across the organization and networks, thereby driving more informed decisions.

Ensuring Fairness in AI Models

As AI becomes more pervasive, ensuring that AI models remain fair and unbiased will be a significant challenge. Platforms will need to develop robust frameworks for detecting and mitigating bias in AI algorithms, conducting regular audits, and maintaining transparency. By leading in responsible AI deployment, platforms can build stronger user trust and differentiate themselves in an increasingly competitive market. Establishing an **AI Center of Excellence** within organizations can centralize these efforts, ensuring consistent practices and ongoing improvement.

Scaling AI for Large Datasets

Scaling AI models for large, complex datasets presents significant challenges, particularly in terms of computation, storage, and cost. Platforms that can develop efficient, scalable AI solutions—through innovations in distributed computing or cloud-native architectures—will gain a competitive advantage by being more adaptable and efficient. This scalability must be supported by **adaptable architectures** that are dynamic enough to change with evolving demands, often described as "living" or "composable" architectures.

Compliance with Global Data Laws

As platforms expand globally, they must comply with diverse data protection laws while maintaining performance. This requires implementing data localization, privacy safeguards, and encryption methods that meet regional regulations without compromising user experience. Platforms that successfully integrate compliance into their operations can expand with minimal friction, offering services across multiple jurisdictions. Leveraging **ecosystem models**—where business, platform, and technology strategies evolve together—will help in aligning compliance with business objectives.

Balancing Automation with Human Oversight

With the increasing automation of platform operations, effective human oversight becomes crucial to ensure ethical decision-making. Platforms that can balance automation with human oversight will not only improve efficiency but also maintain accountability and trust, making them more appealing to businesses and regulators alike.

Reducing the Environmental Impact of AI/ML

The environmental impact of AI and machine learning models, especially those requiring extensive computational resources, is a growing concern. Platforms can mitigate this impact by optimizing algorithms, using energy-efficient hardware, and adopting green computing practices. By focusing on sustainability, platforms can appeal to environmentally conscious consumers and organizations, enhancing their brand reputation and market position.

The Future of Platforms: Evolutionary, Not Revolutionary

The future of platforms will be evolutionary rather than revolutionary, even if that might seem counterintuitive. Imagine a future where quantum computing is abstracted into on-demand infrastructure and new-age chips, enabling 6G exchanges and empowering not just software-based platforms, but also far more intelligent and advanced systems. This would usher in a new era where augmented reality platforms become possible on a level we've never seen before. Thrilling, isn't it?

Organizations that solidify their current platform and technology practices, build the necessary resilience for change, and then lead with AI/ML advancements will be more successful than others. AI and ML architecture patterns will deliver the most benefit if implemented in stages, utilizing more reconfigurable or composable architecture layers. These patterns can be broadly categorized into three types:

Stage 1 - AI/ML Features Integration

This is the most straightforward integration that has already begun and will continue to expand. AI/ML features, in the form of models, services, or micro-features, are increasingly being incorporated into existing platforms. Organizations are leveraging these capabilities to enhance functionality and improve user experience. This stage presents opportunities for organizations to benefit from advanced functionality with minimal investment, allowing them to start building resources and expertise.

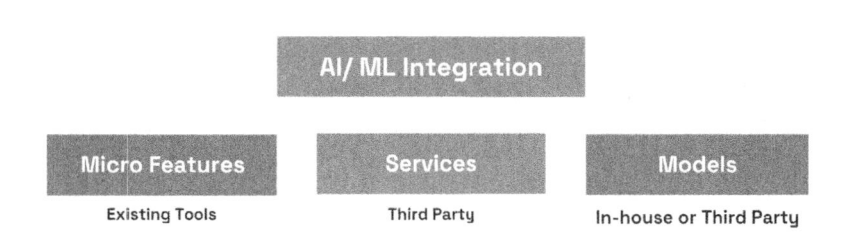

```
                    ┌─────────────────────┐
                    │  AI/ ML Integration │
                    └─────────────────────┘
┌──────────────────┐ ┌─────────────────┐ ┌──────────────────────┐
│  Micro Features  │ │    Services     │ │        Models        │
└──────────────────┘ └─────────────────┘ └──────────────────────┘
  Existing Tools         Third Party      In-house or Third Party
```

Stage 2 - Integration of Intelligent Platforms and Architectures

Looking ahead, integrating intelligent platforms into both legacy and new systems will become increasingly prevalent. This process will involve leveraging existing platforms and services, integrating them into current landscapes to create a seamless, hybrid experience. Future efforts will focus on ensuring compatibility, data consistency, and a unified user experience. While challenges will include overcoming integration complexities and maintaining system harmony, the opportunities lie in enhanced functionality, extended system lifespans, and improved overall performance.

```
Utilizing Third Party
Platforms and Services
        ↓
Integrating into
Existing Landscape
        ↓
Ensuring
Compatibility
        ↓
Ensuring Data
Consistency
        ↓
Creating Unified
Experience
```

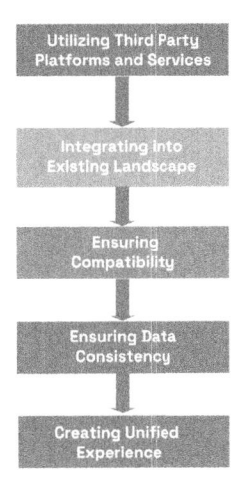

At this stage, the primary challenge will be addressing integration complexities and preserving system harmony. As new functionalities are introduced, it is crucial to focus on extending system lifespans, which will be key to setting up improved overall platform performance and enabling new business patterns.

This layer will greatly benefit from integration flexibility and a well-governed data fabric—attributes that are essential for any platform today or in the future (refer to the definition in Chapter 4).

Stage 3 - Running Your Own AI/ML-Driven Platforms

In the future, organizations will increasingly manage their own AI/ML-driven platforms, requiring comprehensive oversight of machine learning models, operations, lifecycles, and observability. This approach will empower businesses to develop independent platform capabilities, aligning their growth with niche or domain-specific business models. For example, an automotive company might develop its own AI-driven platform to optimize its supply chain, resulting in significant cost savings, personalized car features, and faster time-to-market. Challenges such as the need for advanced expertise and ensuring scalability will arise, but the ability to customize and innovate offers significant competitive advantages.

Successfully running your own AI/ML-driven platforms will require advanced in-house expertise. With a strong focus on scalability, reliability, and platform trust, organizations that excel in customization and innovation will secure a competitive edge.

Full Fledge AI/ ML Driven Platforms

- Comprehensive Features & Operations
- Machine Learning Models & Lifecycle Management
- Robust Observability

The three stages outlined above offer a clear path toward future platforms powered by AI and ML. While these stages might appear sequential for most organizations, their implementation will heavily depend on existing platform capabilities. Mature organizations may choose to work on these stages in parallel, leveraging their advanced platform expertise.

This concludes both this chapter and the book.

To shape the future of your platform, start by gradually building and strengthening your data and information fabric. Combine these efforts with a focus on delivering exceptional user experiences. As you innovate in the current and upcoming eras of platforms, integrating the Platform Success Blueprint is not just an option—it's the most strategic path forward.

Key Takeaways:

- The future of platforms with AI/ML will be evolutionary, emphasizing experience and trust rather than a revolutionary focus on speed and pace.

- Leveraging your current data and information fabric will be crucial to fully harness the potential of these technologies.

- Progressively evolve your usage patterns from Stage 1 to Stage 3, as highlighted above, to stay ahead in the platform landscape.

---

1. https://sloanreview.mit.edu/article/the-future-of-platforms/

Appendix

Appendix A - Chapter Solution Key

Please note that there may be some overlap in the areas of concern, and this is an indicative categorization of questions. If your High, Medium, or Low score on a question falls under one or more of these categories, your concerns will be addressed in the corresponding chapter mapping. However, Sections A and B are must-reads for building a strong foundation and understanding the deeper connections with these areas of concern.

To fully grasp the relevance of this solution key, please attempt the exercise at the end of Chapter 1, then revisit this solution key if you haven't already done so.

S. No.	Area of Concerns	Chapter Mapping
1-42	Platform Essentials and Patterns	Section A and B (all chapters)
20, 31, 39, 40	Platform Success Blueprint and Strategy	Section C and D (all chapters)
2, 33, 18, 26, 17, 41, 42	Core Business Domain and Platform Strategy Integration	Chapter 6 and 7
1, 8, 11, 12, 13, 21, 23, 24, 25, 29, 36, 37	Platform Design, Development and Technology Strategy	Chapter 9, 10, 11
3, 4, 10, 15, 34, 38	Platform and Technology Strategy	Chapter 7 and 9
5, 7, 9, 14, 16, 28, 32	Technology Strategy and Ecosystem Integration	Chapter 9
6, 19, 22, 30, 35	Platform Experience and Economization	Chapter 7 and 8

Appendix B - Prevalent Platform Business Models

In this appendix, we explore the most prevalent platform business models that shape today's digital economy. Each model represents a unique way in which platforms facilitate transactions, interactions, or services across different sectors, supported by real-world examples to illustrate their application.

https://forms.gle/ga7HKJZG5k1Hj5ap8

Appendix C: Essential Platform Templates

https://forms.gle/ga7HKJZG5k1Hj5ap8

Discover a variety of essential platform templates designed to streamline your processes and elevate your platforms. These templates will gradually become available at the path above. Click the link above to download the ready-to-use templates directly from the website.

Appendix D: FAQs (Frequently Asked Questions)

Question 1: What is the difference between digitalization and platformization?

Answer: Digitalization refers to the process of converting analogue information into digital form and using digital technologies to enhance business processes. Platformization, on the other hand, involves the development of digital platforms that connect multiple users—such as consumers, producers, and service providers—allowing them to interact and create value in a shared ecosystem.

Question 2: What is the cloud, and why is it important?

Answer: The cloud refers to a network of remote servers hosted on the internet that store, manage, and process data. Cloud computing allows businesses to access and store data and applications over the Internet rather than on local servers, offering scalability, flexibility, and cost savings. AWS, GCP, and Microsoft Azure are the three leading cloud providers, each with its strengths. AWS is known for its extensive service offerings and mature ecosystem. GCP excels in data analytics, AI, and machine learning capabilities. Microsoft Azure integrates well with Microsoft products and services.

Question 3: What is a hybrid cloud, and how does it differ from other cloud models?

Answer: A hybrid cloud combines on-premises infrastructure (and/ or private cloud) with public cloud services, allowing data and applications to be shared between them. This model provides greater flexibility and more deployment options by enabling businesses to leverage both private and public cloud environments.

Question 4: What roles do platform service integrators play in a platform ecosystem?

Answer: Platform service integrators help integrate various services and technologies within a platform ecosystem. They ensure that different components—such as software, hardware, and networks—work together seamlessly, enabling efficient operations and enhancing the overall user experience.

Question 5: What is the difference between a user, a consumer, and a producer in a platform context?

Answer: In a platform context, a user is anyone who interacts with the platform. A consumer specifically refers to those who use or purchase goods or services provided by the platform. A producer is someone who creates or supplies goods, services, or content on the platform. (More on this in Chapter 4)

Question 6: What are multi-sided platforms, and why are they important?

Answer: Multi-sided platforms are digital ecosystems that connect two or more distinct user groups, such as buyers and sellers, or service providers and consumers. They are important because they facilitate value creation through network effects, where the platform's value increases as more users participate.

Question 7: What does XaaS stand for, and what does it mean?

Answer: XaaS stands for "Everything as a Service," a collective term for services delivered over the Internet. It encompasses various service models, including SaaS (Software as a Service), PaaS (Platform as a Service), IaaS (Infrastructure as a Service), and more, enabling businesses to access and manage services remotely.

Question 8: What is a domain in the context of platform strategy?

Answer: A domain in platform strategy refers to a specific area of expertise or business focus that defines a company's operations. It encompasses the core activities, services, and value propositions that the platform supports and optimizes. (More details in Chapter 5 and 6)

Question 9: What are network effects, and how do they impact platforms?

Answer: Network effects occur when the value of a platform increases as more users join and participate. Positive network effects can lead to exponential growth and success, as a larger user base attracts even more users, creating a virtuous cycle of value creation (more on this in Chapter 4).

Question 10: How do multi-sided platforms differ from traditional business models?

Answer: Multi-sided platforms differ from traditional business models by facilitating interactions between multiple user groups, rather than just focusing on a direct relationship between producer and consumer. This interconnectedness creates value through network effects and can lead to more complex and dynamic business ecosystems.

Question 11: What is platform engineering, and why is it important?

Answer: Platform engineering is the discipline of designing and building toolchains and workflows that enable self-service capabilities for software engineering organizations, particularly in the cloud-native era. It is crucial for creating scalable, efficient, and reliable platforms that empower developers to deliver high-quality software more quickly.

Appendix E: Platform Metrics Model

https://forms.gle/ga7HKJZG5k1Hj5ap8

For readers of this book, a platform metrics model and a range of metrics are available for download at the link above. Explore a collection of essential platform metrics designed to streamline your efforts and get you started. Click the link to download these resources.

Appendix F: How do Platform Users differ from Consumers?

Here's a list of platform users and consumers' roles or engagement levels with platforms: https://forms.gle/ga7HKJZG5k1Hj5ap8

About the Author

Shweta Vohra is an accomplished technology architect with over two decades of experience driving innovation across diverse industries, including automotive, healthcare, travel, and finance. As a double master's degree holder, Shweta has built a distinguished career working with global giants such as Booking.com, Accenture, IBM, and TCS. She is a recognized advocate for women in tech, a patent holder, speaker, mentor, and a trailblazer in platform development, cloud technologies, and AI/ML.

Originally from India and now based in the UK, Shweta believes deeply in the power of technology to drive sustainable change and innovation. Her passion for travel has led her to work for one of the best in the travel and tech industries, Booking.com. Among her favorite travel destinations are Japan and the Lake District in the UK—places she cherishes for their beauty and tranquility.

Through her work and interactions, Shweta strives to deliver meaningful experiences and believes that the true value of technology lies in improving people's everyday lives. This book distills and delivers years of her experience, providing valuable insights to help others navigate the complex digital landscape.